SIN
AS
ADDICTION

Patrick McCormick

New York Paulist Press Mahwah

Book Design: Ellen Whitney

Copyright © 1989 by Patrick McCormick

Library of Congress Cataloging-in-Publication Data

McCormick, Patrick T.
    Sin as addiction / by Patrick T. McCormick.
      p.   cm.
    Includes bibliographies.
    ISBN 0-8091-3064-5 : $7.95 (est.)
    1. Sin.   2. Compulsive behavior—Religious aspects—
Christianity.   3. Catholic church—doctrines.   I. Title.
II. Title: Addiction.
BT715.M374   1989
2411.3—dc19
                                          89-3020
                                           CIP

Published by Paulist Press
997 Macarthur Boulevard
Mahwah, NJ 07430

Printed and bound in the
United States of America

Contents

To Barbara and Bill who deserved a book on grace

1

■

The Mystery of Sin:
A Crisis

■ ■ ■

Strange Silence: New Voices

We are in the midst of a storm over sin. In a place
where there used to be clear and evident terms,
precise definitions and rather universal consensus we now
find ourselves confronted with confusion, ambivalence and,
often enough, a puzzling silence. Only a short while ago the
subject of sin seemed to constitute the whole of Catholic
moral theology. Morality and sin, particularly of the sexual
sort, kept company like love and marriage. Yet today morality in the pulpit and print seems strangely mute on sin, at
least when compared with the attention it received a scant
two or three decades back.

Nowhere is this silence or muteness so deafening as in
the confessional box. Lengthy lines every Saturday after-
noon have been replaced by small groups gathered twice a
year for Advent and Lenten penance services. At the heart
of all this silence seems to be a general confusion about what
sin is, or more concretely what actions are "still" sins. For
when asked about this change of practice, people speak
about not having anything to confess, about not feeling the

1

need to go to confession, or about not thinking that the things they used to confess "are sins anymore." Even when middle-aged Catholics raised on weekly or bi-weekly use of the sacrament come to confession after a six month or one year absence they often begin by saying that they really don't have any sins worth mentioning. One wonders what all those folks used to talk about on Saturday afternoons, but more importantly one wonders what sin is.

And it is not only the sudden silence we find so unsettling. Adding to our confusion is that what words we do hear about sin sound so strange and foreign to the Catholic ear. In place of the tried and true sermons on the seven deadly sins or the sins against the ten commandments, we now hear priests attacking a new breed of sins like racism, consumerism, militarism, neo-colonialism and, of late, sexism. Our bishops write letters speaking about "sin-of-the-world," "structural sin," and "social sin." Political and liberation theologians speak to us about the need to address the "sinful" economic and political structures of oppression, and some Christian pacifists have argued for the need to exorcise missile silos. We find ourselves asking, "What is going on?"

As a result of all of this Karl Menninger's cry has become, "Whatever became of sin as we used to know it?" Sin has moved out of the bedroom and into the boardroom. The sin of stealing from the workplace has been replaced by that of economic oppression. Indeed, for many a Catholic, hearing recent episcopal and papal statements on sin in the social setting has probably been like the confusion of running into an old and unfamiliar acquaintance at the mall. We recognize the face, but cannot quite place the name.

In the midst of all this turmoil one is also surprised to note that while our clergy may not talk as much about sin as they used to, there is a new wave of interest in this question on the part of secular authors. Scott Peck's *The People of the Lie,* Karl Menninger's *Whatever Became of Sin?,* Henry Farlie's *The New Seven Deadly Sins,* and Erich Fromm's *The Anatomy of Human Destructiveness* are just a few examples of psychologists and essayists attempting to rescue some good in the midst of this crisis. For those of us more accustomed to hearing about the religious notion of sin in the confines of a church or theological text this switch seems curious. But maybe not. It could be an indication of the profound need to wrestle with this very human mystery.

Some Reasons

What is at the root of all this trouble? With a crisis as major as this one there will be as many explanations and theories as persons confronted by the issue. Some of these answers seem less probable, others pose interesting questions and bear some investigation.

Clearly sin has not evaporated. Contrary to the opinion of some, it has not disappeared like some adolescent case of acne which we outgrew as we moved into adulthood. Whatever else has happened, sin, with all its malice and destructive power is still in our midst. Even a glance at the evening news reveals the persistent presence of a human malice and evil which stymies the imagination and can frighten the most hopeful soul. Sin is still in town. Instead, what seems to have occurred is a shift in what many call our "sense of sin." At risk is not the existence of sin but our ability to grasp and say something articulate about the presence of sin in our lives and world.

Is this because the human race in the latter part of the twentieth century has shucked its conscience? Is it enough to say that the sin of this generation is simply that it has lost its sense of sin? That the advances of technology and science have given humans a sense of immortality and godlike power which renders us arrogant, unaware of our limits and ignorant of our relation to the divine? Or is it because the "sexual revolution" of the 1960's has deadened our sense of the immorality of casual, uncommitted and recreational sex? Or could it be that the rampant and materialistic consumerism of our society has anesthetized us to the wrongfulness of selfish and gluttonous lifestyles?

While there may be real truth in these assertions, they do not seem to sufficiently explain the current crisis. For if we are so blissfully unaware of our own sinfulness, where is all this language on social and structural sin coming from? What are all those homilies and encyclicals on the arms race, oppression and ecology about? No. It is not simply that we have lost our sense of sin, for the notion has been introduced into areas traditionally devoid of much moral analysis. Instead of anesthetizing us, the issues of social and structural sin have provided a prophetic call raising, not lowering, the moral consciousness of Catholics.

Others have suggested that in the changes of the Second Vatican Council Catholic moral theology has turned its back on a profound sense of sin. Some contemporary theologians are accused of paying insufficient attention to this very fundamental concept of morality. In attempting to overcome some of the notable excesses of a classical theology of sin, some have argued that contemporary theology has thrown out the baby of sin with the bathwater of legalism and juridicism.

While there is no doubting that Vatican II set a new course for moral theology, the heart of this course was not a rejection of sin but a call to deepen our understanding of the mystery of salvation, including the mysteries of sin and grace. The shift in post-Vatican II moral theology moves us away from a strict reliance upon "act-analysis" to one that takes seriously the moral character and story of the human person. Further, it calls us to pay attention to the insights of biblical and systematic theology, as well as the evidence of the social sciences. By doing this we have come to recognize the superficial and unsatisfying character of the traditional grasp of sin as an individual act performed in violation of the laws of God, church, or human nature. The turn to the subject has pushed the grasp of sin closer to its roots in the human heart. At the same time there is little doubt that these developments have meant some real confusion as the models for such a fundamental human mystery undergo change and flux.

While there are many possible explanations for the present turmoil and confusion, it would seem that the most likely is that we find ourselves in a crisis of models. We have lost confidence in the images and models we use to grasp and explain sin. For the developments of the past several decades have confronted us with new insights and information, even new categories of thought. In light of these our understanding of the reality of sin in our lives, our community and our world can no longer be adequately expressed with traditional models. Like old garments the previous models cannot be stretched to fit the new cloth. They tear and rip at seams. They are inadequate, progressively less relevant, and woefully inaccurate. We need new models.

But isn't this trivializing the present turmoil? Why would a crisis of models be so important? How could it generate the confusion and the shifts in practice we have noticed? Are models of sin so significant?

We can only speak about or understand the basic mysteries of human existence through the use of models and imag-

ery, and sin is a fundamental mystery of our existence. We
cannot define sin, at least not ultimately. We cannot mount
it on a specimen slide and slip it under a microscope. We
cannot diagram it as we would a sentence in English class.
Through the art of our theological language, which Thomas
Aquinas told us was always analogous, we can use the models and images of metaphor and simile to point at, describe
or evoke the mystery of human sinfulness. When those images and models begin to fail us, when we can no longer
grasp or express the reality of sin through traditional models,
we are in the midst of a serious crisis.

Such is our present situation. For at the present time the
classical models which have for centuries explained sin to us
have fallen into real disrepute. The theological and anthropological developments of the past few decades have raised fundamental questions about the suitability and accuracy of these
models. Sin has not gone away, but the language and models
which have provided access to a coherent and comprehensive
grasp of sin are becoming progressively less helpful.

Sin: A Mystery

People writing on the subject of sinfulness have noted
time and time again that this is a fundamental mystery of the
human experience, an important point for the present discussion. It is important because we need to know what we mean
by the assertion that sin is a mystery.

Sin is not a mystery because it surprises or puzzles us, as
it most surely does. For the fact that the human person, as a
child of a gracious and loving creator, has the capacity, even
the tendency to turn in freedom to the doing of real evil
seems a tragic and puzzling irony. This irony is only deep-

ened by the recognition of that capacity and tendency in (nearly) all human beings. That we do the evil we would not do haunts the human psyche and conscience. That we are so pervasively drawn to do that evil stymies us.

But this tendency is not merely a puzzle, it is a basic datum of human experience, and indeed of revelation. Sin is a basic part of who we are. Throughout our story human persons in every epoch and culture, of every ethnic and racial group, of every creed and nationality have freely chosen evil and often blatantly inhuman behavior. They have chosen to sin. Nor do we experience this evil only in the hearts of others, but in our own as well, or even especially there. We have met the enemy in the mirror over a toothbrush. And in the eyes in the mirror we have seen some deadly attraction to do more and more evil, to sin more. We experience this evil in actions, in consequences, in powerful and deadly attractions, in frustrating and anguishing resistance to the good in ourselves, in others and in the very structures of society.

Models of the Mystery

When Elizabeth Barrett Browning tried to evoke for others the mystery that was her love she turned, like Paul, to imagery and models. In attempting to speak articulately about the evil of sin, about its origins, its nature, its character, indeed in order to describe the evil which has so much power over us, we too reach out for the tools of analogy and metaphor. We employ models and images to gain access to this mystery.

Such models are helpful, but they continue to be analogous language. They are not the evil itself, nor is any one of them (or, indeed, any combination of them) capable of fully capturing or describing this mystery. It would be better to think of all of these models as pointers guiding us in the direction of a fuller grasp of the mystery of sin, but hardly offering a final and accurate definition.

In the case of sin our models must in some way speak about the issue of a terribly fractured relationship with God into which the human race has stepped and from which it needs to be redeemed and forgiven. Models of sin need to address the freedom and lack of freedom which persons experience in the decision to turn away from God and in lives radically affected by that decision. Such models also should reveal the way in which this sinful mystery engages and cripples human freedom, comes to rest in and perverts the human will, and is expressed in destructive and deadly actions, which we call sinful. Finally, such models have to speak about the malice and destructive power which sin manifests in so many and varied ways.

No model or even set of models can adequately perform such a series of tasks. Nor could any model consistently offer the best insights into the nature of the mystery of sin. Instead, models represent the best efforts in a particular context and out of a particular worldview to point to this mystery, to illumine it in our minds, and to give us a handle on understanding it. But the task taken up by these tools is never-ending. Thus, as our grasp and insights develop there is a need for newer and better models. This means that we are to be constantly re-evaluating the models we employ.

Resistance of the Mystery

In the case of sin there are some special reasons for attention to models. The first is that the mystery of human sinfulness, as the narrator of John's gospel reminds us, "hates the light." The malice of the human heart does not want to be understood, to be grasped. Sin hates the truth and loves the lie. Thus, it will be particularly difficult to speak clearly and adequately about this fundamental human mystery, so resistant to the light of truth. There is a special danger here that models will be chosen which do not come to know the truth, but which cooperate with sin, whose angelic sponsor has been called "the prince of lies."

The second problem is even more insidious. We are sinners. We lack any real objectivity on this issue. Not only does sin hate the light, but we too try to hide in every crevice. We are corrupted and weakened by this moral illness and find ourselves in the unhappy position of being wounded healers. We are willing, even happy, to take the speck out of another's eye, but slow to approach the plank in our own. Scott Peck has called this the heart of evil, the unwillingness to suffer moral pain, to accept the truth about ourselves, the need to lie.

These facts make the quest of adequate models of human sinfulness both urgent and difficult. The mystery of human sin, especially in our hearts (and institutions), resists serious scrutiny.

Sin and Grace

But that is not the whole story. Sin is a fundamental human mystery, but not the only one. Grace, too, is part of this story. Indeed, it is the more important part, the center. As Paul has put it, "where sin abounds, grace abounds all the more." The mystery of human sinfulness, at least for the Christian, must be studied in the light of the redeeming and salvific grace of God, which means that the models and language we employ to describe sin must not obscure the real presence of God's redemptive and merciful grace in the human story. Sin is to be understood in the context of salvation. The models of sin are to express the real tragedy of this mystery, but not to cooperate in a spirit of despair that would speak the lie that sin is the last word in human history. C.S. Lewis has a number of wonderful images in *The Great Divorce* in which he describes the puny awfulness of sin. So too, our moral theology must refrain from employing models that stress the reality and power of sin as greater than the mercy of God. This would be sinful.

Sin: Looking at Some Models

So, models and images are the tools with which we apprehend and speak about the mystery of human sinfulness. But at the present moment we are, so to speak, between models. The contemporary storm over sin is in large part due to a crisis of models. Theological and anthropological reflections have led us to raise serious and damning questions about some of our traditional understandings of the reality of sin, and we have not yet developed a consensus about satisfying substitutes. We are not ready to move forward and yet we cannot afford to remain or regress. This explains both the continuing silences and our ongoing confusion.

And yet we need to do something. It is necessary to critically examine a number of models of human sinfulness—both those which have fallen into trouble and disuse of late as well as those being tentatively proposed in light of recent developments. By doing this the weaknesses of the first group may offer us the basis for a standard with which to judge the second.

While images of sin abound, it would seem that three basic models have traditionally dominated our consciousness of sin.[1] This triumvirate has tended to understand sin from a cultic, juridical or subjective perspective. Accordingly, sin has been described in these models as (1) a stain, (2) a crime, or (3) personal. While these models have much to recommend them, the present crisis indicates a failure on their part to adequately express the mystery of sin, and/or to convincingly call people to conversion from this evil.

Therefore, after a brief sketch of the history of the concept of sin, we will examine and critique in some depth these traditional models, hoping to discover in their weaknesses some keys to a better "sense of sin."

We will then examine three other, somewhat experimental models in an exploratory attempt to articulate some correctives to the limits discovered in the first three. Sin will be described as (1) a spiral, (2) a disease, and (3) an addiction. No one of these models is intended as a definition of the mystery of sin. Instead they are offered primarily as correctives to some of the excesses and limits of the first three and as tentative steps in a continuing journey towards the truth.

Notes

1. In traditional moral theology human sin has usually been spoken of as "mortal," "venial," and "original." In the recent past the distinction between the first two categories has been seen as too sharply defined, so some theologians have added the term "serious" to describe acts of sin that

were not light but fell short of being ultimately deadly. For the most part this sort of language has been employed primarily to describe the notion of "personal sin." While this language continues to be useful within set limits, it fails to adequately express the full breadth of the experience of human sinfulness. It also rests upon certain assumptions (often unspoken) about the nature of sin. For these reasons it would not be fruitful to critique or rework these categories. Instead, it will be necessary to look at some of the basic models of sin which underpin these three (or four) terms.

2

■
■

THE STORY OF SIN

■   ■   ■

In this chapter we will draw out the rough lines of a
■ brief historical sketch of the development of the notion of sin. However, before reviewing the history of this
concept within the Judeo-Christian and Catholic traditions,
it will be necessary to make four introductory remarks.

First, sin is a mystery. While this point is obvious
enough, it tends to bear repeating, especially in light of any
attempt to sketch a history of this idea. The richness and
depth of human experience of sin defies easy definition and
transcends the limits of language. Thus we will discover in
the following history numerous attempts to grapple with and
understand sin, each one tending to focus in on various elements and facets of this deadly reality. Successive generations employed a range of terms and models in attempts to
describe distinct characteristics of the sin experience. Some
of these models were more complete or appropriate than
others, but none of them communicated the full reality of
sin. At their very best they could but point in the direction of
this mystery, offering a key into understanding.

Furthermore, sin is a religious notion. The idea of sin
situates our conversation in a religious context, pointing specifically to the relation of the human person (and/or commu-

nity) to the divine. Sin refers to some disruption threatening the health or survival of that relationship. Therefore, sin-talk is ultimately linked to God-talk. To speak of sin is to speak about humanity's relation to God. Hence sin is not reducible to being understood in exclusively ethical language about good and bad or right and wrong. While it does have a real moral dimension, sin is more than unethical, immoral or illegal activity. Sin is unholy.

Third, the study of sin has always been carried out by sinners. There is a sense in which this should invite us to both caution and humility. For sin is not simply an object we can view under a microscope. It is a virus from which we suffer and which affects our heart and mind and soul in our quest for the truth. John has told us how sin hates the light of truth, and we know well ourselves how resistant we are to such light once the conversation about our own sinfulness turns suddenly concrete and specific. Although we need a sense of our own sinfulness, it is essential to recognize that the history of this concept has been affected by the sinfulness of humanity.

Finally, sin is but a shadow to grace. It is too easy to be mesmerized by sin in all of its terrifying might, to be sucked into the darkening vortex. When studying sin one needs to remember that this evil is a paltry (though deadly) parasite compared to the power and liveliness of grace. We investigate this parasite not because of any intrinsic worth it has, but so that we might better understand and cooperate with the gracious and life-giving medicine of God's redemptive love. Our aim here is therapeutic. Our basis is faith.

Old Testament: Roots and Shifts

It would be impossible to discover a single understanding or theology of sin in the Old Testament.[1] Instead we are confronted with a number of efforts to speak about the mystery of human sinfulness in a variety of contexts and from several points of view, each of which attempts to highlight or underscore distinct characteristics of this notion.

However, such a tapestry of images is not without certain patterns or directions. There is evidence of some ongoing development and reflection in which different aspects of the notion of sin come to be better and better articulated. Unfortunately, there is also some indication that other notions tended to be over-emphasized or under-emphasized, leading to an unbalanced or poorly developed understanding of the reality of sin. After a brief presentation of some basic terms, we will attempt in this section to draw out some of the lines of development as well as deterioration, focusing in on three major shifts which took place in the Hebrew grasp of sin.

Diagnosis: Naming the Sin

It would be a serious error to assume that the concept of sin has been univocally understood in the Judeo-Christian tradition which reaches back over three millennia. Just as serious would be the mistake of thinking that one single notion of or word for sin dominates the story of Judaism or Christianity. Instead we are confronted with a number of terms of varied origins and meanings which are employed to express several different aspects of the mystery of sin.

Therefore, we begin the study of the Hebrew understanding of human sinfulness with an examination of the terms the Hebrew uses to speak of this mystery. Such an etymological approach is clearly limited, but it is capable of at least introducing us to some basic insights into the way in which the notion of sin was understood. By attempting to understand the root meanings of such terms, as well as the way these originally secular words were applied and understood in the religious context of the covenant, we may get a view to a fuller grasp of the Hebrew concept of sin itself.

No single Hebrew word stands behind every translation of the English term "sin" in scripture. Instead, several words are used to get across an understanding of the idea of sin, words with different roots and meanings. In order to initiate an investigation into what the Old Testament was talking about when we read "sin" today it will be necessary to look briefly at three of these words.[2]

"Hattah" and its cognates represents the dominant Hebrew translation for "sin" in the Old Testament. Originally a secular term meaning "to miss," as in "missing the mark," this word found a new and slightly different meaning in the religious context. Here "hattah" referred to the failure to meet an obligation or to observe a duty owed someone in a relationship. Thus it came to mean the failure to be faithful to one's duty to the covenant. In this way "hattah" meant not only to sin, but to sin *against* the one owed the duty. Thus the term focused in on the fact that sin is against Yahweh and the covenant which constitutes Israel.

"Awon" refers to a state of being twisted, crooked or bent. It points to a defect of character or a disorder which is experienced as a burden or a weight under which one moves and from which one hopes to be freed. In the religious context this idea would point to the fact that sin is experienced as a burden which one carries and which might be handed over to another in expiation, as in a sacrifice or to a scapegoat. In this way the term came to highlight the experience of sin as guilt.

"Pesha," on the other hand, has the root meaning of rebellion. It refers to the rising up in conflict against the given order. In the convenantal setting this would be seen as a profound act of rising up against Yahweh, of being disloyal, of hardening in malicious opposition against the loving mercy of Yahweh.

These three terms, as well as others, represent different ways in which the Old Testament authors speak about the experience of sin. The presence of a plurality of terms points to the fact that "sin" was not understood univocally. Instead the word referred to numerous insights and dimensions of the human experience of this mystery.

From the Unholy to the Illegal

The earliest roots of a consciousness of sin are grounded in dread. Various authors have written about a pre-ethical stage in which the sinner is one awakened to an awful sense of being unclean by a confrontation with the Holy. Here the Holy is experienced as terrifying and wrathful, often seeking vengeance for some human violation of the sacral dimension. By contrast, being a sinner is the experience of being profoundly unholy.

This consciousness of sin is considered to be pre-ethical because it is normally the violations of the religious cult alone which produce the wrath of the Holy.[3] Sins tend to consist primarily in the actual and external breaking of the cultic taboos, regardless of the intent of the "violator." Notions of moral consciousness or subjective culpability are foreign. Significant alone is that there has been a rupture in the cultic harmony.

Such "sins" of unholiness are associated with the sacral dimension of the life of the community, items like cultic purity, sexual conduct and the laws of worship. The reference points tend to be where the sacred touches the secular, or, more likely, where the secular is forbidden to touch the sacred.

This sense of sin as "unholy" dominates the earliest Hebrew understanding. Israel often experiences itself as impure before the holiness of Yahweh. The cultic laws of Leviticus or the "law of holiness" provides ample evidence of this. Persons are punished for transgressions of the cultic law without reference to their intent.

What is most striking, however, for our investigation is not the lack of an ethical perspective at this level of development, but rather the profound and abiding presence of a sense of being unworthy or unholy before the "face of God." This sense, which ultimately finds an inadequate expression in dread or fear before the wrath of an implacable god, is the heart of a developing and utterly profound awareness of the disordered relationship between humanity and divinity. It is this sense of the sacred, or the sense of being alienated from the sacred, which grounds the notion of sin so deeply in the completely religious soil of the covenant.

As the theology of the covenant develops there is a gradual incorporation of the moral dimension in the understanding of sin. Sin comes to refer more and more to a willful and conscious violation of the relationship of the covenant by the people of Israel (and later by individual Hebrews). The "sin" of Israel is no longer equated with a failure to attend to the external demands of the cult. Instead, it refers to an internal stance of being unfaithful, rebellious or hardhearted before the call of the law and the prophets.[4]

Another development of this period is that the moral dimension begins to include behavior not normally considered to be directly related to the sacral. At this stage in the Hebrew understanding "sin" also referred to the unjust treatment of the neighbor, especially the widow, the orphan, and the foreigner. Such concerns are normally part of the ethical field of analysis.

The classical prophets of Israel are often offered as examples of this level of development beyond an exclusively ritualistic grasp of "sin." While there is much truth in this analysis, it would be unfair to split Israel's cult and morality too cleanly. For the prophet too calls the people to be holy, and chastises them for their infidelity (which he describes as adultery and fornication) to the covenant. Furthermore, the "law of holiness" included references to the treatment of the neighbor, while the prophets described justice and mercy as characteristics of "true holiness" and "proper sacrifice."[5]

The point here is that although there is discontinuity between these stages, there is also profound continuity in the notion of sin as grounded in the religious experience of the covenant. For in the covenant persons are radically connected to the untouchable and yet unbelievably loving God of holiness. Sin is that which violates or ruptures the covenant, an experience not well understood or articulated at the more primitive level, but radically experienced.

Even in the shift to the moral stage there is a move beyond taboo without a loss of the sense of the sacred. Instead, there is a fuller articulation and understanding of the implications of this experience of the unholy encountering the Holy. The moral concerns of the prophets about a just treatment of the neighbor, as well as the growing import of subjective intentionality, have their meaning against the backdrop of the religious world of the covenant. These later insights tended to unpack the fuller meaning of the awfulness of sin as a profound severing of the covenant with the Holy.

Unfortunately, development is often enough accompanied by deterioration. The shift beyond a narrow and exclusively cultic grasp of the covenantal relationship is followed by a tendency to retreat from the demand of the Holy by building a wall of laws and regulations by which humans could pretend to define the character of their relationship to mystery. The post-exilic move toward a spirit of legalism focused more and more attention upon the arid details of the law, and less and less upon the profound experience of sin as rupture, as alienation, as death in the face of life. As this understanding grew the notion of sin tended to focus more and more upon "sins" merely as transgressions of the law, acts separate from the covenantal experience and the mystery of the sacred.[6]

From Corporate to Personal Sin

In the contemporary mind sins are committed by individual persons. The ancient Hebrew would find this concept quite foreign. Sin in the Old Testament was seen originally as the unfaithful response of the people of Israel to the demands of the covenant.[7] Israel sinned as a people, and was chastised, punished, and called to repentance as a people. The notion of personal responsibility or culpability came as a relatively late development to Jewish thought. Such a position may seem unacceptable to a western mind planted so deeply in the soil of individualism, but it is clearly the position of the earlier writings of the Old Testament. Sin was the act or stance of the whole community of Israel, by which it ruptured the covenantal relationship in which it stood to Yahweh.

The reason for this position is simple enough. Israel is

convenanted to Yahweh as a people, not as individual persons. Therefore, salvation or condemnation, life or death, redemption or perdition are covenantal and thus national issues. Sin is that which threatens or weakens the covenant, that which threatens the very identity and survival of the people of Israel. The one threatened by sin, indeed the one who sins, is Israel.

At the same time there is a progressive realization that Israel sins through the transgressions of persons, that there are concrete and specific manifestations (lists of sins) of the sin of Israel, and that individual persons do indeed commit such "sins."

There is also a progressive realization of the character and importance of the individual's role and responsibility, meaning a recognition of the possibility of personal sin and punishment. The idea of personal responsibility for one's own sins or of being culpable or punished only for the sins one has personally committed finds its clearest voices in the work of Jeremiah and Ezekiel, who first suggest that God does indeed not punish the children for the sins of their parents, and that each person will receive a punishment only for the actions he has committed, and not for those of his ancestors.[8]

However, the recognition of individual responsibility and culpability should not be equated with the denial of corporate sin. To assert that Israel discovered the reality of personal sin does not imply that communal notions of sin are either outdated or antiquated. Such an assumption ignores the social dimension of the human person and acts in profound ignorance of the communal character of humanity's covenant with God. The meaning of sin includes the personal without denying the social or abandoning the more basic covenantal dimension of life.[9]

From Experience to Act

Israel's original understanding of sin, as described above, was rather undifferentiated.[10] The primary focus was upon the experience of being in dread before the Holy, an experience which told the sinner that something was very wrong. As a result of this focus on the sin-experience, the primitive Hebrew notion of sin tended to include more than those willful and personal deeds of rebellion which the contemporary mind understands as (actual) sins. For the Israelite sin also meant all of the various elements of the broader experience of being in sin, including especially the consequences of sinful actions.

With the development of ethical thought there was a gradual shift in focus. At this point sin came more and more to be understood as residing in the willful rebelliousness of the personal subject and in the deeds which expressed this sin. Sin shifted from experience to transgression. With this shift came a developing grammar for sin, distinguishing all the various elements of the originally undifferentiated totality, interpreting the experience of wrongness as the consequences of sin proper.

Some Directions

What we observe in an analysis of the Old Testament evidence is that the original understanding of sin, rooted in the experience of the covenant, begins as fairly undifferentiated and moves in stops and starts in the direction of clearer articulation. Sometimes this movement is development, incorporating new insights into a rich vision. At other times the grasp of sin seems to become more sterile and abstract, paying too high a price for clarity.

Progressively there is a development of the notions of personal responsibility and moral accountability. The experience of sin is better explained in the light of free choices made in one's heart about the call of the covenant. Catalogues of sinful deeds identify the ways in which the rebelliousness of persons or a hard-hearted people is expressed. There is also the maintenance of an awareness of the reality of the sacred and covenantal dimensions of sin. The move to the personal and the moral are not away from the covenantal and the sacred, for sin is a convenantal and religious reality.

Sin is thus understood in two fundamental ways: first, as a radical sense of alienation, a rupture in the covenant which constitutes the very existence of Israel, and, secondly, as the willful decisions through which the people (and then individual persons) choose to act out or deepen that state of alienation.

New Testament: SIN and Sins

The Ministry of Jesus

The life and ministry of Jesus makes it clear that he came into the world to save humanity from the power of sin. From his temptations in the desert, through a life proclaiming the kingdom of God and a message of repentance, healing, and forgiveness, to his death and resurrection, Jesus comes to face the question of sin in all its wrath and fury.

The New Testament presents Christ's response to sin characterized by (1) a profound awareness of the power and deadly malice of sin, (2) a radical and universal call to conversion (metanoia) away from sin and toward the kingdom, and (3) an offer of forgiveness to person(s) entrapped in the snares of sin.[11]

Even the most cursory reading of the New Testament reveals a sense of the inimical stance between the kingdom and the power of sin. Christ has come into the world to face this reality and to free humanity from its burden through the proclamation of the kingdom of God. The language of the gospels reverberates with the awful power and reality of sin. Jesus confronts this power as it corrupts and enslaves all sorts of persons, hardening their hearts to the good news of the coming of God's kingdom and turning them in dramatic violence against Jesus.

The response of Christ is to call persons to conversion, to challenge them to "sin no more" or to leave lives of sin behind them and to "come, follow me." This challenge is offered individually and corporately to Jew and Gentile. All are invited to imitate the grain of wheat and die to the power of sin, being born again into new and eternal life. Sometimes the word is gentle and warm (the woman at the well, the woman caught in adultery), sometimes it is a hard and stark word of challenge (calling the Pharisees blind and hardhearted). But it is a call to a radical transformation which can only be compared to dying and being reborn. However, this metanoia refers not only to legal observance or cultic purity, but calls instead for a broken and contrite heart converted to the Lord. For the transgressions (sins) which persons commit are rooted in their "hardness of heart" (sin), and it is from the latter that one must be converted.

Probably the most striking feature of Jesus' response to sin was his attitude toward the sinner. Again and again the incredible compassion of Jesus for the outcast and alienated

sinner comes to the surface, whether in his parables of forgiveness (the prodigal son) or in his own actions (dining with
tax collectors and prostitutes). He reveals here a commitment to those imprisoned by their own sinfulness, a commitment to offer them a word that will heal and forgive.

John and the World

Although we continue to find in the New Testament a
strong awareness of the notion of personal sin, it would be a
serious error to conclude that the highly privatized grasp of
sin which dominates western culture finds its roots here. For
while the gospels speak of sinners and their sins, there is
another use of the term which points to a broader, more
corporate grasp of the reality of sin.[12]

"There is the lamb of God who takes away the sin of the
world." In this early passage of the fourth gospel (1:29) the
Baptizer announces the coming of the one who not only will
remit all of our individual sins, but will actually take away the
sin of the world. The use of the singular here points to a sense
of sin which moves beyond the limits of the personal experience of the act of sin. In his description of a world which is
willfully and maliciously hostile to the message of the gospel,
John speaks of a reality of sin that is transpersonal. The world
which Jesus came into and which decided to know him not,
which decided to resist his word and harden itself against it,
represents not just the sins of persons, but SIN.

This notion of SIN is more than the concrete and conscious decisions to turn against the kingdom, to do and be
selfish. John is speaking here of a state of hostility that precedes, tempts, and infects the will of the individual. SIN
refers to a state of enmity between the word of God and the

world. There is in this theology of sin some primal stance of rebelliousness against God's will, some awful and terrible state in which persons who sin find themselves.[13]

Paul and the Flesh

It would be difficult to imagine a disciple whose wrestling with the notion and experience of sin has been more influential than that of Paul. His letters are rife with profound insights into and rich reflections upon the experience and mystery of sin. Like John, he offers an analysis of sin which includes but moves beyond the conscious and free acts by which persons choose to turn away from God.

Perhaps the most striking image in Paul's theology of sin is represented by the term "flesh." Like the "world" in John's gospel, flesh refers not just to the physical dimension of life, but to a larger and fuller experience of the whole person in which there is a hardening resistance to the word of God. Paul speaks of a SIN which saps and mocks his will, pressing him to do the evil he would avoid and leading him away from the good he would do.

SIN in this understanding represents a power which permeates the human condition and saps man of his will to listen to the gospel call. Such SIN is more than the individual acts of rebelliousness committed by men. Instead it represents the ground from which this rebelliousness springs.[14]

Directions

The New Testament period offers us a sense of sin located in the context of a call for total conversion and an offer of mercy. The profound gravity of sin is experienced not only in personal transgressions or even individual hard-heartedness, but also in a transpersonal, perhaps cosmic, sense of malicious resistance to the proclamation of the kingdom.

Sin and the Church

Sacraments and the Law

The story of sin in the Christian community after the New Testament period is probably best told in the context of two sacraments: baptism and penance. For it is in attempting to deal with the church's sacramental role in reconciling or forgiving sin and sinners that much of the significant writing on this subject has its roots. And later it will be around such issues that Catholic moral theology will formulate much of its writings on sin.

In spite of this sacramental focus the study of sin in the western church tended to be dominated by legal analysis. Pastoral concerns about sin evolved into discussions concerning the gravity of matter and subjective culpability.

Baptism and Original Sin

With the gradual inclusion of the practice of infant baptism in the first centuries after Christ different authors came to ask what purpose was served in offering baptism to those (infants) who could not possibly have committed any personal sin. Since such persons were incapable of such acts, would they not be innocent of sin, thus rendering baptism unnecessary in their case?

The developing response of Christian authors was that in such cases baptism removed from such persons the stain or mark of the sin of Adam, an original sin in which all persons, insofar as they were descended from the first parents, shared.

Augustine offers the most articulate version of this position, and he does so in response to Pelagius' assertion that grace is not absolutely essential for salvation. Augustine asserts that all persons suffer from the effects of the fall of Adam, and that all are thus in need of redemption from the disordering reality of this sin. While original sin is different from personal sin in that the individual is not culpable for the former, there is still a real need for baptism to liberate the newborn from the power of this sin and to fight the effects of this sin, found in concupiscence.

The theology of original sin continues to find its development in the scholastics (Thomas' Summae: Ia IIae; Q.81–85) and later at the Council of Trent, where it received its formal definition and was taught in a stable form for better than three centuries. Within the notion of original sin several questions surfaced and were treated at some length, questions referring to the source of the sin, its relationship to personal (mortal) sin, the means by which it is transmitted from one generation to another, whether all persons suffer its effects, and indeed what its effects were. In the Council of Trent the bishops offered several basic assertions about the truth of original sin. Among these were the following:

1. Adam sinned in a concrete and specific action, and through this act sin entered into the world.
2. The sin of Adam is communicated to all human-

ity through sexual reproduction, so that every
human person (save Christ and the Virgin) is
truly a sinner before any conscious act of the
will.
3. Baptism completely removes the guilt imputed
to man from this sin, while the effect of concupiscence remains in him.[15]

Confession and Venial or Mortal Sins

Even within the New Testament there is evidence of
some variation in gravity or seriousness among different
sins.[16] Not every act in which a person chose to turn away
from God was of the same weight or import. Some decisions
were taken more seriously and tended to reflect a more
deadly condition than others. For example, John asks his
fellow believers to pray for their fellow sinners, except in the
case of "deadly sin," for which he does not invite them to
pray. Furthermore, so serious is the sin against the Holy
Spirit that it shall not be forgiven (Mk 3:28; Mt 12:3lf; Lk
12:10).

In the early centuries of Christianity the practice of public penance was developed for and offered to those sinners in
the community who had been baptized and then fallen from
grace. However, not every person who sinned was expected
to embrace such a discipline. Only those who had committed
one of the big three—apostasy, adultery or homicide—were
commanded to seek the rather strong medicine of public
penance. For those "regular" souls who sinned through
lighter and less serious actions, the Christian authors recom-
mended a recitation of the Our Father, some fasting, and
works of charity for the poor. By such actions could one

overcome or be forgiven such minor or easily pardonable sins.[17]

Thus there is a recognition that not every sort of sinful act is of the same weight or import. Instead, one sees in the penitential practice an assertion that some sins are rather easily pardonable through personal prayer and works of piety, while others are of such a serious nature that one needs to turn to the church's discipline of public penance.[18]

This unfolding distinction between serious and light sins was based on both the gravity of the objective "matter" of the transgression as well as the subjective culpability of the sinner. A sin might be less serious because of either the relative insignificance of the act in question or the impeded freedom of the subject.[19]

As time passed concern about these distinctions led to the development of the categories of mortal and venial sins, which achieved some formal definition at the Council of Carthage (418).[20] Indeed, as the discipline of public penance was replaced by the practice of private confession, which then came to be the ordinary means of doing sacramental penance for one's sins, juridical concerns fueled a growing obsession with "mortal" and "venial" sins. The former needed to be confessed in species and number, while confession of the latter was optional.

Although these categories reflected a biblical insight into a gradation of sin, Bernard Häring has expressed some alarm over the fixation which grew up around such distinctions and the often scrupulous attempts to define them. The desire to accurately determine whether sins being confessed in penance were mortal or venial sometimes overshadowed a call to conversion from all sin.[21] This and other distinctions revealed the growth of a tendency to analyze sin from a legal or juridical viewpoint, a trend that continued with the birth of the discipline of moral theology. By the period of the scholastics moral analysis had become somewhat fixated on developing a syntax for sin, distinguishing between sin and its punishment, mortal, venial and original sin, material and formal sin, as well as sin as act and sin as state. Theologians discussed the questions of concupiscence and sin as a privation of habitual grace, and drew up a catalogue of seven capital sins. Under the influence of this rather abstract and juridical approach clarity was often enough gained at the cost of a more pastoral and biblical sense of sin.[22]

Sin and Moral Theology

In large part the "science" of moral theology as it was known previous to Vatican II was rooted in various attempts to train clergy in the administration of the sacrament of private confession. In light of this the analysis of sin tended to be governed by the two juridical concerns of determining the guilt of the penitent and assigning a just penalty. No two movements highlighted these concerns better than the penitentials and the manuals.[23]

The Penitentials

With the development of the practice of private confession by Celtic monks spreading the gospel through western Europe in the early middle ages we find the introduction of a new kind of Christian work, the penitentials. Written for an uneducated confessor, the penitentials sought to offer a practical and pastoral guide to the assignment of penances based upon the sin confessed in the sacrament.[24]

Thus the penitentials were lists of penances to be assigned according to the sin committed. Not theological or pastoral works in any real sense, they nonetheless exercised profound influence upon the practice of confession and later Christian thought about sin and forgiveness. Through these texts Christian morality took a big step toward a minimalistic legalism which defined morality as an avoidance of sinful activity, and (implicitly) grace as the absence of sin.

The penitentials focused inordinate attention within the sacramental setting not upon the forgiving grace of God, but on the number, species, type and gravity of sin. In this way Christian morality shifted in the direction of becoming a science of sin.

The Manuals

In the sixteenth century another major work appeared in the newly distinguished field of moral theology. Moralists writing for pastors hearing the confessions of their parishioners composed texts which aimed at assisting in the determination of the genus, species, seriousness, nature and number of the sin(s) confessed. These manuals of moral theology focused inordinate attention on sin with little or no insights from the tradition of dogmatic theology or sacred scripture. Such texts were more connected to the tradition of canon law and came to understand and explain sin(s) rather exclusively from the legal perspective.[25]

The problem with the manuals was that they tended to define the entire field of moral theology within the confines of the study of sinful actions, and they did this without any significant reference to the message of the gospel. Extensive treatises upon the multitude of sins in all their genus, species, number and nature rendered moral theology a science of sin, and not a particularly graceful one.

Contemporary Shifts

Well into the twentieth century Catholic reflections on sin were formulated in the context of penitential practice and characterized by a high degree of abstract and juridical analysis. The extensive syntax of sin focused rather exclusively around the act analysis of individual transgressions. Even here primary import was given to the objective matter of such deeds, relegating questions of subjective culpability to a secondary status.

However, in the years since the Vatican Council some major shifts rooted in movements over the past century and a half have begun to blossom. Moral theology is in a period of flux, characterized by both growth and confusion. The manuals have been abandoned and differing sorts of methodological approaches to the study and teaching of Catholic morality are being experimented with. Not only new answers but new questions and new voices are being heard.

Concerning sin these changes have meant a number of shifts.[26] The harshly juridical analysis of the past is being replaced by a more pastoral approach rooted in the loving mercy of God. Rediscovered covenantal language from scripture has tended to underscore the relational, vocational and personal dimensions of sin. Insights from depth psychology and Thomistic studies have led to attempts to articulate a theology of sin based less on act analysis and more on an understanding of virtue and vice. More systematic reflections have better grounded moral theology's understanding of sin in the context of grace and conversion. Social analysis and the experience of global injustices have led to a recapturing of biblical notions of the corporate dimension of sin.

Much of what has occurred has been creative and helpful, and it would be an unfair and unrealistic criticism to note that moral theology has not yet attained a new synthesis. Instead the present state reflects a developing pastoral field struggling to be better connected to scripture, dogma and the secular sciences, as well as more focused on a call to conversion. To say that moral theology in general and our grasp of sin in particular is in crisis is not necessarily negative. Such a crisis is also an opportunity for new growth. To this end we will now turn to an investigation of a series of models which have been and might be employed in our quest to better grasp the mystery of sin.

Notes

1. Alphonse Spilly, "Sin and Alienation in the Old Testament: The Personalist Approach," in *Chicago Studies*, vol. 21, no. 3, 1982, 212.

2. Bruce Vawter, C.M., "Missing the Mark," in *The Mystery of Sin and Forgiveness,* Michael Taylor, ed. (New York: Alba House, 1971) 24. James Gaffney, *Sin Reconsidered,* 1983) 15–16.

3. Paul Ricoeur, *The Symbolism of Evil* (Boston: Beacon, 1967) 25–44. Kevin Condon, "The Sense of Sin," in *Irish Theological Quarterly,* vol. 49, no. 3, 1982, 160–164.

4. Spilly, "Sin and Alienation," 212.

5. David Kelly, "Aspects of Sin in Today's Theology," in *Louvain Studies,* vol. 9, Fall 1982, 192. Condon, "The Sense of Sin," 162.

6. John Coventry, "Sixteenth and Twentieth Century

Concepts of Sin," in *The Way Supplement,* vol. 48, Fall 1983 51–52. Piet Schoonenberg, *Man and Sin: A Theological View* (Notre Dame: University of Notre Dame Press, 1965) 98–99.

7. Coventry, "Sixteenth and Twentieth Century Concepts of Sin," 51.

8. Schoonenberg, *Man and Sin,* 102. Henri Rondet, *The Theology of Sin* (Notre Dame: Fides, 1960) 12–13.

9. Coventry, "Sixteenth and Twentieth Century Concepts of Sin," 51–52.

10. Vawter, "Missing the Mark," 27–29.

11. Rondet, *The Theology of Sin,* 22–29.

12. Franz Böckle, *Fundamental Moral Theology* (Dublin: Gill and Macmillan, 1980) 85.

13. Timothy O'Connell, "A Theology of Sin," in *Chicago Studies,* vol. 21, no. 3, Fall 1982, 279–280.

14. Rondet, *The Theology of Sin,* 29–35.

15. Schoonenberg, *Man and Sin,* 157–177.

16. Schoonenberg, *Man and Sin,* 25–28.

17. The Council of Elvira (300–305) noted a distinction between more and less serious offenses when it did not demand entry into the order of penitents for every sin, requiring instead a period of abstention from Communion for lighter transgressions (canon 21; Mansi 2:9).

18. Paul Palmer, *Sacraments of Forgiveness* (Westminster: Newman Press, 1957) 67. St. Augustine, *Faith and Good Works* (PL 40:227f).

19. A letter of Leo the Great (440–461) to Rusticus of Narbonne distinguishes among sins based upon the matter (Ep. 167; PL 54:1209). Felix III (483–492) makes a similar distinction based on the freedom of the sinners (Ep. 7; PL 59:925f).

20. Schoonenberg, *Man and Sin,* 27–28.

21. Bernard Häring, *Free and Faithful in Christ,* vol. 1, 396–398.

22. Eugene H. Maly, *Sin: Biblical Perspectives* (Dayton: Pflaum/Standard, 1973) 2. Rondet, *The Theology of Sin,* 66–68.

23. James Gaffney, *Sin Reconsidered* (New York: Paulist Press, 1983) p. 61.

24. Bernard Häring, *The Law of Christ,* vol. 1 (Westminster: Newman Press, 1961) 10.

25. Häring, *The Law of Christ,* vol. 1, 18–19.

26. James Hug, "Social, Cultural Healing," in *Chicago Studies,* vol. 23, no. 3, Nov. 1984, 33–35. Norbert Rigali, "Sin in a Relational World," in *Chicago Studies,* vol. 23, no. 3, Nov. 1984, 321–332. Peter Henriot, "The Concept of Social Sin." Piet Schoonenberg, *Man and Sin.* Louis Monden, *Sin, Liberty and Law* (Sheed and Ward: New York, 1965).

3
■
■

SIN AS STAIN: THE DEFILEMENT MODEL
■   ■   ■

LADY MACBETH. Yet here's a spot . . . Out, damned spot! out, I say! One: two: why, then 't is time to do't. Hell is murky. Fie, my lord, fie! a soldier, and afeard? What need we fear who knows it, when none can call our power to account? Yet who would have thought the old man to have had so much blood in him? . . . The thane of Fife had a wife; where is she now? What, will these hands ne'er be clean? No more o' that, my lord, no more o' that: you mar all this with starting . . . Here's the smell of blood still: all the perfumes of Arabia will not sweeten this little hand. Oh, oh, Oh! . . . Wash your hands; put on your nightgown; look not so pale; I tell you yet again, Banquo's buried; he cannot come out on's grave. (Macbeth: v/1)

T he passage above from Shakespeare's tragedy of
■ murder presents us with the dreamwalking Lady Macbeth acting out the deep and "murky" guilt she feels for the murder of Banquo. What is most striking about this sleeping accusation is the imagery of blood-soaked hands

which Shakespeare uses to communicate the pervasive and unwilling sense Lady Macbeth has of her feeling of blame, of her sin. Hands stained and fetid with the ooze and stench of blood point not only to the act of crime, but to a deeper and even more awful sense of unease, even dread before the wrath that is to come. For intermingled with her frantic efforts to scrub out the "damned spot" of her murderous complicity is a profound sense of terror about being punished (in "murky" hell) for this heinous crime.

Shakespeare has, in the lady's bloody and unwashable hands, found an image that resonates to the core of the human psyche, that touches the spine of the soul and plays hauntingly upon memories beyond the reach of the free and conscious intellect. We see in her unconscious and desperately futile scrubbing some mirrored echo of a sense memory within ourselves and our consciousness, a reminder of evil's contaminative and deadly power pre-dating the ethical or legal notions of sin and guilt. There is a touch here that cannot be reduced to the rational, but that speaks of the mystery and origins of the human grasp of evil.

Nor is the bard alone in his use of this imagery to speak about a primary, if somewhat primitive, sense of human sinfulness. Literature and scripture alike are both rich with passages describing sinful or guilty humanity as tainted, stained, marked, rendered unclean and/or impure through some violation of the holy or sacred.[1] The sinner is often described as contaminated by some unclean quasi-physical, quasi-spiritual liquid which seeps through the defenses of his virtue and renders him guilty. God speaks to Ezekiel in such language.

> Son of man, when the house of Israel lived in their land, they defiled it by their conduct and deeds. In

my sight their conduct was like the defilement of a
menstruous woman. Therefore I poured out my
fury upon them [because of the blood which they
poured out on the ground, and because they defiled
it with idols] (Ez 36:16–17).

Common to these various descriptions of human sinfulness and guilt is a language of defilement. In some way
humanity is evil or at fault, and this is experienced as being
defiled, corrupted, stained by the murky, contaminative and
corrosive power of the unclean, the unholy. Sin is not so
much or only an act as it is a raw experience of terror symbol-
ized by a blemish, a mark of defilement.[2] In this ancient and
primitive model sin is a stain.

Bram Stoker's *Dracula* offers a classical and poetic illus-
tration of the "stain" model in his use of the imagery of
contaminative and tainted blood marking those it touches
and rendering them unclean. But it is in Leviticus 11–16 that
one finds the fullest and clearest thematic articulation of this
vision. In these six chapters the author develops the notion
of sin as stain and sinner as tainted, including a number of
concepts related to and growing out of this way of understanding human sinfulness.

From examining these and other illustrations we discover that the language of defilement presumes a number of
things about our understanding of sin. Some of these pre-
sumptions find real resonance with our deepest convictions
about the fundamental character of human malice, while
others seem at odds or inconsonant with a more developed
notion of sin. Thus, while the image of sin as stain may
indeed be ancient and original, it is not so clear that such an
image continues to be true or useful. In order to evaluate
this model it will be necessary to unpack it somewhat, review-

ing its presuppositions and implication, and critiquing its
strengths and limits. We turn to this task.

Defilement and Contamination

In the stain model of sin there is a sharp sense of the
difference, even the separation, between that which is good
and that which is evil. The standard or measure of that separation is expressed in the language of *clean* vs. *unclean,* or
pure vs. *impure.* This is the language of defilement. The
person or community has defiled itself, rendered itself guilty
in the face (especially) of the one who is clean and pure, in
the face of the holy. The sin separates one from the holy by
rendering one unclean. The mark or stain of this "unclean-
ness" expresses well the character of sin as that which renders one separate, even inimical to the good. For defilement
is more than the weight of guilt. It includes both a sense of
terror before the wrath of the holy as well as revulsion toward the self now seen as unholy.[3]

This stain model, therefore, understands the sinner as
discovering his/her sinfulness in the experience of being defiled before the face of God. Sin is experienced as a sense of
profound dread and unease before the holy, a sense that
something is very terribly wrong. Like Isaiah in the temple
decrying that he is a man of unclean lips amidst a people of
unclean lips, the sinner discovers his/her defilement in the
context of facing the holy. This unholiness is expressed as
defilement, as being unclean or impure. The sinner is one
who is not able to face or enter into (and certainly not to
touch) the dimension of the holy because he/she is unclean.
In many ways the stain model is associated with a sense of
being ashamed and in dread before the accusing face of the

holy. On some primitive level traces of this is operative in the fall narrative in Genesis, where the man and the woman experience a profound shame/dread before the holy that walks among them.

According to the stain model the defilement of sin is contaminative. This is true in two ways. Defilement often occurs in this model when persons have touched or been touched by something forbidden. Violations of taboos normally take place through some form of unlawful touching. Secondly, the one who has sinned must be isolated from the camp lest it or someone else be defiled by contact with him/her. The language of the stain model is strongly tactile. This is seen in so many of the proscriptions of Leviticus 11–16. Moral evil, which is not so clearly distinguished from physical evil, is, in this model, a powerful and deadly contaminant.[4] Mere contact can render a person tainted or impure, and the laws of Leviticus make it clear that it is indeed the touching of the unclean which constitutes sin in this model. Those who touch dead bodies, are touched by the flow of body fluids, or touch (eat) unclean foods are contaminated by these touchings and thus rendered unclean and impure.

All of this presents us with an image of moral evil as a contamination of the person which is achieved through simple, even casual contact with objects in the world that humans are not to touch. Such contact renders the person unclean, and hence unfit to enter into the realm of the sacred. The one defiled is to be removed from the camp of the Israelites, cannot enter into the celebration of ritual, and is forbidden entry into holy places. The blemish of their sin renders them unholy in the sight of God. The imagery of a stain resulting from contact with some murky liquid of evil captures well this sense of defilement. Leprosy becomes such an apt metaphor for this moral evil because it is a

contaminous disease which evokes dread due both to its terminal character and because it is so repulsive. The leper is
not only contaminated, but also profoundly unclean and
threatens to contaminate others.[5]

A Pre-Ethical Model

Even upon so brief an inspection it becomes obvious
that although such a model hauntingly reveals some of our
most ancient and lurking suspicions of the nature of sin,
poetically and symbolically reaching beyond the dead and
dry legalism of much traditional teaching on this topic, there
are some problems here.

The stain model of sin is pre-ethical in three fundamental ways. While ethics may not be the only context in which
one needs to speak about sin, since it is primarily a religious
term, the fact that there are (at least) three areas where the
stain model has not achieved the level of ethical thought is a
serious criticism.

To begin with, the stain model of sin does not distinguish between voluntary and involuntary action.[6] Instead,
accidental or inadvertent actions are also counted as sins, as
long as they violate the proscriptions of the laws concerning
the clean and the unclean. This is seen most clearly in numerous passages of Leviticus, chapters 4–5, where those who
have sinned by accident or inadvertently are directed to offer
sacrifice in atonement for these sins. The fact that there is to
be atonement makes it clear that the distinction between
formal and material sins would not apply to this early level of
understanding.

According to this model, therefore, we are not ultimately concerned with the intention of the agent who has

chosen freely to reject the covenant of Yahweh. Instead of focusing in on the interior will of the sinner, the stain model addresses (as primary?) the experience of being defiled as a result of having (intentionally or not) violated the taboos of one's relation to the holy. Sin as taboo violation represents a pre-ethical grasp of moral evil, one that has not seriously or sufficiently considered the import of the intention of the subject.

Nor does the content of the proscriptions of the stain model of sin coincide with a developed and ethical grasp of that which is morally wrong. To begin with, the stain model forbids or defines as sinful numerous sorts of actions which today we would consider as irrelevant to a moral code. The notion that contact with the dead or with women giving birth could render one unclean and sinful makes no sense to and might even offend the conscience of a contemporary ethical person. The extraordinary focus upon and centrality given to matters ritual and/or sexual is characteristic of the stain model and would be rejected or at least countered by those who understand moral rightness as equally concerned with matters interpersonal, societal and cosmic.[7] Indeed, the very absence of a deep or abiding concern for such questions of interpersonal and social justice renders the stain model inadequate to deal with a broad range of serious ethical and moral questions, questions that both the classical prophets and Jesus argued were essential to the achievement of true holiness. Furthermore, even when one discovers within the stain model proscriptions against interpersonal crimes such as homicide, the grounding of such proscriptions tends to be on cultic and ritual arguments instead of ethical ones. The shedding of blood is against a reverence for the sacredness of this life-force instead of a violation of the dignity or sanctity of the neighbor.

A third way in which the pre-ethical character of this model shows up is on the level of motivation. Dominated by defilement and shame language, the overriding experience of this model does not tend to underscore the rightness or wrongness of an action. Instead it speaks of the subject's experience of terror and dread before the avenging wrath of the holy in response to the violation of some taboo. Like Lady Macbeth, it is the murkiness of hell's punishment which renders her murderous activity so evil. One is sorry simply because one is going to be punished in such an awful way.[8]

In line with this Ricoeur has noted that the stain model reveals a consciousness which cannot distinguish clearly between the order of moral and physical evil. The experience of suffering implies that there has been some offense which must be paid for, while the action is seen as an offense primarily because it has led to a punishment. This tight and unnuanced association of physical and moral evil is characteristic of the pre-ethical grasp of sin present in this model.[9]

Grounded in the Holy

While the model of sin as stain may not be fully ethical it is completely religious. Defilement language is grounded in the experience of the self as unholy in the face of the holy. Thus, the model of sin as stain is grounded in a sense of the holy, of the sacred. To sin is to be unholy and to be unholy is to sin. Having said that, however, one needs to ask more about what it means to be unholy. It is only through an understanding of the notion of the unholy that one can fully grasp the notion of sin expressed in defilement language.

The holy is dreadful. As previously noted stain imagery tends to present a profound separation of good and evil in the language of clean and unclean. This antithetical approach underscores the radical over-and-againstness of the God-human relationship, presenting the sinner as one who experiences the holy not only as different, but even as a threat to continued existence. The holy cannot be viewed or touched; the sacred is that which is experienced as mysterious, threatening, ominous. This dread is revealed in the extreme caution with which the holy and indeed the realm of the holy is to be approached. One is to take off one's shoes, offer sacrifices and holocausts, undergo rites of purgation and lustral washings in blood or water. One is not to touch. Indeed, the holier a reality is, the more untouchable it is. The appropriate response to the holy is a sense of awe, of fear, perhaps even a sort of terror.

In some sense the holy is to be feared because it is so mysterious, so far beyond the grasp and control of humans. The sacred describes the dimensions of life which are not malleable to human touch, not responsive to human machinations. Instead, the holy is precisely that which is beyond the pale of human authority. The sacred is that which cannot (or should not) be manipulated by humans.

The realm of the holy, therefore, describes those realities over which human beings do not have dominion. Instead, the holy is that which comes under divine mandate alone. For the primitive believer operating on this level humans are out of their element and in violation of the holy especially when addressing the mysterious questions of life and sexuality. In these areas taboos keep the wandering person from entering the realm of the sacred.

Indeed, a brief review of Leviticus illustrates that this model ascribes an untouchable character to the mystery of human sexuality and to the vitality of human life, especially in association with vital body fluids like blood and semen.

When persons came into contact with such fluids or such mysteries they were considered unclean and needing of purification. When such fluids were spilled or poured out, or even when they passed from a person, they were considered to be impure and in need of atonement. Sex and life, represented by these fluids, were mysteries beyond the grasp of mortals and so to touch them was in some sense to intrude upon the holy.

The many proscriptions concerning the wide variety of diseases associated with leprosy also reveals how the mysterious is identified with the divine in this model. The fact that these diseases were of unknown cause, incurable and terminal meant that they were beyond the pale of human control. Not being able to understand or control them meant that they were ascribed to divine origin and commonly interpreted as punishment for sin. The temptation to see incurable diseases as an expression of the avenging will of the holy is quite common, though one of our own generation had forgotten until quite recently.[10]

Because of this vision of the world as divided between the holy and the unholy, the stain model defines that which is sinful quite differently than a secular or even religious ethicist might. Stain and defilement language continues to operate primarily upon the level of taboo, defining that which is unholy as evil, and establishing what seems like very arbitrary standards for the realm of the holy.

The Need for Cleansing

Once it is accepted that sin is understood primarily as a stain rendering one unclean and thus unfit for contact with the holy, the logical conclusion would be that ritual cleansing constitutes the response to this impurity. And this is indeed what we find. Rites of cleansing or purification take on three basic forms in the scriptural literature: lustrations, purgative sacrifices or oblations, and rites of expiation.

The rites of lustrations, ritual purifications of persons in preparation for entering into a holy place or feast, abound in the books of Leviticus, Exodus and Numbers. The people, or the altar upon which a purification sacrifice is to be offered, would be sprinkled with blood or water in order to wash away their impurities and uncleanliness. Such ritual washings symbolize the experienced need to cleanse oneself of the taint of sin which cries out for atonement. Perhaps one of the best known examples of this tight association between sin/stain and the need for washing can be found in Psalm 51:7:

> Purify me with hyssop until I am clean
> wash me until I am whiter than snow.

Baptismal rites in which the sinner is called to bathe in the life-giving and cleansing waters, while moving beyond the stain concept of sin, are clearly grounded in such imagery. Even the deliverance of the Israelites at the passover takes place through the sprinkling of blood on their doorposts.

It is important to note that ritual cleansings serve not only to remove the stain of sin, but also as a preventive against contamination. The multiple washings and rites of lustration are not only to purify the sinner, but also to keep the innocent untouched by the contaminative power of evil.

Purification, however, need not come through the washing in blood or water. When Isaiah speaks of being a man of unclean lips an angel of the Lord is sent to cleanse those lips with the fire of a live coal. Fire, too, can have a purifying effect, purging the blemishes of sin through burning. This is clearly operative in the popular conception of purgatory, where the stains of non-mortal sins are burned away from the soul of the believer. It is also operative in the very notion of a sacrificial holocaust in which the gift offered is made sacred in the fiery oblation.

Finally, the blemish of sin invites expiation, a response of atonement in which the sin and stain are wiped away, undone through some sort of sacrifice or penance. This expiation is often associated with exile, removal from the community or the dimension of the holy. The exile can be ended only when an appropriate sacrifice or cleansing has taken place. In expiation we are referring primarily to the sinner in some way undoing the results of his/her offense against the holy, and returning to the original state of order or balance in the universe.[11]

Indeed, what is so noticeable about this model is that since the grasp of sin remains ultimately in the external dimension, so too the response fails to invite conversion. Also, since the understanding has assumed an automatic response of punishment for the (sometimes unintended) violation, there is little serious attempt to look for mercy or forgiveness from the holy. The holy remains completely mysterious and unapproachable. The most which can be hoped for is a mollification of the wrath of the holy by offering a clean sacrifice or a rite of purification. By making such an offering it is hoped that the sinner will be able to re-enter the dimension of the holy.

Later Development

What is perhaps the most interesting characteristic about the grasp of sin as strain is its flexibility and tenacity. The previous discussion has highlighted the roots and original matrix of notions associated with this concept. Stain was conceived in a pre-ethical, ritualistic and external grasp of moral evil. However, as richer and fuller understandings of ethics and moral truth developed in the religious and faith traditions, the concept of clean/unclean and pure/impure continued to be employed, sometimes being reworked and given new and fuller meaning, sometimes not. The call for ritual cleanliness is replaced in the prophets and Jesus with a call for clean hearts, stressing the need to internalize one's morality. The original association between contact with blood and sin is enriched and deepened with the rage against the shedding of innocent blood. And the unclean spirits who confront Jesus in the scriptures are not ritually impure but morally evil and diabolical. All of this indicates a certain degree of flexibility in stain imagery, which allows it to be reworked into a more internalized and ethical vision of the notion of sin. Whether such flexibility indicates that this model offers an appropriate place to begin doing a Christian theology of sin is yet another question.

Some Reflections

After examining the basic structure and essential elements of this model it is necessary to offer a few reflections upon the strengths and weaknesses of the notion of sin as stain. Much of this critique will rest on an attempt to discover basic tendencies and directions set by this model, evaluating these tendencies in the light of a Christian reflection upon the mystery of sin.

A major problem with this model is related to its unbalanced stress upon the contaminative power of evil, and its implicit assertion that such evil is to be addressed primarily through extrinsic ritual actions oriented to placate a wrathful holiness. The implicit assertion of such imagery is that at very best only a holding action can be fought against evil, that the good has no real power of its own, and that the holy is experienced more as a threat than a help, indeed, the help.

The notion of evil which Jesus confronts in the religious leaders of his time reflects much of the stain model. People are profoundly aware of the power of evil to contaminate and poison their hearts and render them unclean. Thus they expend great energies either avoiding all contact with that which is unholy or cleansing themselves from any intentional or unintentional touchings of such unholiness. This fixation with innocence, actually a sort of pseudo-innocence, is in radical opposition to the one who not only regularly broke the rules of holy times and places, but broke bread and ate (a profound sort of touching) with the unclean and the unworthy.[12]

Fear characterizes such imagery, fear of sin and fear of God. The unholy is understood as so powerful that only avoidance or purifications will keep it at bay. This fear is pathetic in its ignorance of the redemptive and transformative power of God's forgiving grace. It is tragic when such a fear calls persons to become isolated from their all-too-human neighbors, abandoning them to condemnation.

Defilement language too easily becomes fixated on the threat against the self, either from the wrathful holy one or from the contamination of evil. In either case the sinner is an unprotected victim standing between two hostile forces which need always to be appeased or avoided. There is no room here for a profound faith in the holy one who is known as abounding in mercy, filled with generous fidelity and love. There is little or no sense of the power (contaminative?) of the grace of

God or of the importance of forgiveness as a means of transforming a reality tainted by sin.

A second serious limit of stain imagery has been its tight association with sexual taboos. Several authors point to this connection, and there is little doubt about the damage this has done. In the first place defilement language has tended to represent sexuality poorly and in a severely unbalanced manner. The tight association between sexuality and defilement continues to surface in the popular connection between the realms of sin and sex.[13] Sexuality has been too often understood as a tainted and sinful activity. Nor can there be any serious doubt but that at the very least the thrust of this association in the stain model has been oppressive and sexist. The mystery of birthing and sexuality has more often than not been employed to oppress women and associate them and sexuality with some primordial sort of "temptation" about which men have a marvelous sort of pseudo-innocence. Penalties associated with sexual taboos tend to be significantly tougher on women.

This unbalanced focus upon the so-called sacral dimension of sexuality has tended to render religious ethics based upon the stain model blind in the face of questions related to interpersonal and societal justice. The absolute fierceness with which sexual taboos are defended is too often glaring when contrasted to the moral deafness to a prophetic call to justice for the anawin. Sexuality is an important, even fundamental dimension of human life and religious morality. It is, however, somewhat of an obsession of this model.

The model of sin as stain represents an ancient and poetic set of insights into an original experience of the wrongness of moral evil. There is certainly a strong sense here of the real awfulness of sin. In the light of contemporary reflection, however, the model reveals serious limits and handicaps, tending to be extrinsic, fearful, even somewhat fatalistic in its response to moral evil. There is too little sense of the interiority of sin, the power of grace, the mercy of God, or the transforming reality of forgiveness.[14] Instead, we are confronted with a model which seems too narrow in its grasp of the content of sin and too negative in its grasp of the holy. Stain would not be a good model to serve as the cornerstone of a theology of human sinfulness.

Notes

1. Aquinas raises the question as to whether or not sin causes an enduring stain on the soul, which he answers in the affirmative. Ia IIae q.86. In *The new Baltimore Catechism No. 3* (Francis J. Connelly, 1943) illustrations of the soul tainted by sin show a black mark or stain, an image familiar to generations of Catholic school children.
2. Paul Ricoeur, *The Symbolism of Evil* (Boston: Beacon, 1967) 25–44. Louis Monden, *Sin, Liberty and Law* (New York: Sheed and Ward, 1965) 4–8. Alphonse Spilly, "Sin and Alienation in the Old Testament," in *Chicago Studies,* vol. 21, no. 3, Fall 1982, 212.
3. Kevin Condon, "The Sense of Sin," in *The Irish Theological Quarterly,* 159–160.
4. Ricoeur, *The Symbolism of Evil,* 28–35.
5. Shenson, "When Fear Conquers," 34–38.
6. Monden, *Sin, Liberty and Law,* 5.
7. Ricoeur, *The Symbolism of Evil,* 28–29. See also the discussion of masturbation in Karl Menninger, *Whatever Became of Sin?* (New York: Hawthorn Books, 1973) 31–37.
8. Louis Monden, *Sin, Liberty and Law,* 5.

9. Ricoeur, *The Symbolism of Evil,* 25–44.

10. Ronald L. Numbers and Ronald C. Sawyer, "Medicine and Christianity in the Modern World," in *Health/ Medicine in the Faith Traditions,* Martin E. Marty and Kenneth L. Vaux, eds. (Philadelphia: Fortress Press, 1982) 137–140. Douglas Shenson, "When Fear Conquers" in *The New York Times Magazine* (February 28, 1988) 34–38, 48.

11. Monden, *Sin, Liberty and Law,* 5–6.

12. Ibid., 154–156.

13. Robert O'Connell, S.J., "The Sense of Sin in the Modern World," in *The Mystery of Sin and Forgiveness,* Michael J. Taylor, S.J., ed. (New York: Alba House, New York, 1971) 4–6.

14. For a discussion of the limits of a "sacral" sense of sin cf. Bernard Häring, *Sin in the Secular Age* (Garden City: Doubleday, 1974) 15–36.

4
■
■

Sin as Crime:
A Cry for Punishment
■   ■   ■

Q. 158 "What is actual sin?"
A. 158 "Actual sin is any willful thought, desire, word, action, or omission forbidden by the law of God."
Q. 161 "What is mortal sin?"
A. 161 "Mortal sin is a grievous offense against the law of God." (Francis J. Connell, *The New Baltimore Catechism No. 3,* 1943)

The definitions above reflect one of the most if not ■ *the* most, dominant models of human sinfulness, sin as a crime. Thomas Aquinas notes in his discussion of sin (1a2ae, q.71, art. 6) that it is "fittingly defined as a word, deed, or desire which is against eternal law." And, indeed, this notion of sin as being a transgression of the law of God is a constant theme in theological discussions of the reality of human sinfulness. As Henri Rondet notes, "Sin is a fault, a violation of the moral law, a transgression of the divine law."[1] In one of the versions of the Lord's prayer, we ask the Lord to forgive us our "trespasses" as we forgive those who "trespass" against us. In all of this we have the overriding sense of sin as an action in which a person chooses freely and "willfully" to rebel against the God-given order of reality, especially as this order is expressed in divine and natural law.

While "stain" and defilement language may represent the most primitive grasp of human fault, the notion of sin as a crime and the sinner as a criminal has, until the very recent past, clearly constituted the most dominant understanding of human sinfulness. The corrective changes introduced into Catholic moral theology by Vatican II were to a great deal motivated by a sense of profound dissatisfaction with the juridical and individualistic understanding of Christian ethics which not only gave disproportionate attention to the notion of sin, but also tended to understand it exclusively from a legalistic perspective. According to the crime model, sin was seen primarily as the concrete act of a free, conscious and competent individual who had decided (in this act) to rebel against the law of God by being disobedient to one of the mandates of eternal or moral law.

The model of sin as a crime includes three basic assertions: (1) that sin is to be understood primarily in a juridical, even a penal context, (2) that the one who sins is the individual, and (3) that the act of sin is primarily one of willful rebellion, usually the rebellion of a lawless individual against the divinely sanctioned order. This means that the crime model will tend to stress certain characteristics in its presentation of sin, especially the freedom and individuality of the sinner-criminal, as well as the need to punish this willful and forbidden activity. Given the legal and juridical perspective such a model also tends to understand sin primarily as a violation of laws which mediate a necessary order of justice.

Within the crime model, therefore, sin will be understood as an act of willful disobedience, expressed in the

breaking of a law and inviting some sort of just punishment
or desert.

For crime describes not only an action which is against
the laws of the land, but one of such seriousness that it war-
rants a public accusation, judgment, and some sort of civil
punishment. As Dostoyevski and Menninger have noted sepa-
rately, crime and punishment are paired terms, the first crying
out for the latter. (Indeed, the root word for crime may indeed be the same as the word for scream, reminiscent of
Abel's blood crying out for vengeance and illustrative of the
association between crime and accusation.)

Crime: Individualistic and Juridical

The crime model is not specific to Roman Catholicism,
but can be found in various Protestant communities and sur-
faces in different historical periods of the Hebrew covenant.
Indeed, such a model exists in numerous religious communities and traditions. At the same time, however, this model,
characterized by profound individualistic and juridical tendencies, was until very recently the primary model of human
sinfulness operative in Catholic moral theology.

While it is not easy to explain in any real depth the
diverse factors which have made crime such an attractive and
powerful model, it is possible to sketch out a couple of the
historical trends and developments which have contributed
to the dominant sway that juridical and individualistic categories have held over moral theology, and in a special sense
moral theology's grasp of sin. Primary among these have
been (1) the nearly exclusive emphasis upon the individual in
western analytical thought, (2) the intimate relation between
ecclesial and political structures in western Christianity, (3) a

tendency in religious ethics to move away from an original and relational grasp of morality and to develop toward a more rigorous and often rigid legalism, and, most importantly, (4) the practice of the sacrament of private confession in the west.[2]

Western Individualism

The genius of western analytical thinking has been its ability to grasp "essential" reality by abstracting from the flow of cause, context and consequence. Through analysis western thought has focused on those elements within human experience which distinguish, separate and sometimes isolate, thus developing a startlingly clear, if myopic, vision of individual elements of reality. In scientific studies this has meant tremendous growth in a calculative and manipulative knowledge within countless fields of specialization. However, it has also meant a profound loss of a sense of the whole, the cosmic, the unity and interrelatedness of all experience. In political and social thought the west has placed a nearly exclusive stress upon the importance of the individual, tending to see the social or communal sphere only as a limit or threat to that individual. Although this stress has only progressively moved toward including an appreciation for the dignity and work of *all* individuals, western thought has produced extraordinary political documents and institutions respecting and preserving the right of the one over and against intrusion by the many. Western political thought rests on the cornerstone of the inviolability of the individual human being. It does this, however, at the cost of having ignored the reality and experience of human communities, or at the very least of having a severely under-developed grasp of these realities.[3]

Within moral theology in the west it is not at all surprising that these tendencies have contributed to an understanding of sin which is individualistic and privatized. The radical individualism of the west has severed the individual's sin and the sinning individual from the weave of history and society. The free and unconnected will of the separate person, and the expression of that will in particular acts of sin, have often become the sole twin concerns of Catholic morality. Act-analysis and an evaluation of the individual person are the primary tasks of this view of moral theology. Thus, the individualism of the west renders its moral theology compatible with a legalistic framework and a criminal model. For three central concerns of the juridical procedure—(a) the determination that a crime has been committed, (b) ascertaining the culpability of the defendant, and (c) assigning appropriate penalties—represent the major focal points of much of western moral theology.[4]

Church and State

The intimate and often enmeshed interrelationship between church and state which characterized much of the story of Christendom from Constantine to the Enlightenment had a particularly interesting effect upon the notions of sin and crime. The particular history of Christianity as it became a recognized and then the official and mandatory religion of the Roman empire is one in which the borders between church and state were often, and for various reasons, either poorly defined or completely absent. With the progressive deterioration and collapse of the empire, bishops often took on the administrative tasks and roles of magistrates while other ecclesial officials began to assume more and more of the responsibilities reserved to civil authorities in a more secular context. These developments, indeed the whole story of Christendom, with its intermeshing of civil and religious authority, had significant effects upon the concepts of sin and crime.

These twin concepts of religious alienation and civil transgression either came to be seen as roughly equivalent or were employed as interchangeable analogies of one another. Civil government, which claimed religious and moral authority as well as legal jurisdiction over its subjects, argued that any transgressions of the laws of the state were likewise to be considered as immoral and irreligious acts.[5] At the same time religious authority employed sanctions against serious sins which resulted in rendering the sinner an "out-law" in the civil dimension, effectively denying the individual access to the protection or privileges of citizenry. In short, excommunication by the church rendered a person a criminal, which was the specific intent and power of that sanction.

It is interesting to note that this intermeshing of civil and religious authority, also present in the early and pre-secular Hebrew understanding of Israel, had a similar effect upon the understanding of sin. In pre-Davidic Israel there is no distinction between the law of God and the law of the state. Israel was a theocracy, and as Emil Brunner notes,

> The law of the state was at the same time the law of the religious community and the law of the religious community was the law of the state. The laws of religion and the synagogue were enforced by the same coercive means as those of the state, and transgressions of them punished in the same way as transgression of the civil law.[6]

So it is not surprising for us to find the notion of sin as a transgression of the (covenantal) law already present in Hebrew scriptures.

The fact that the interchangeability of these two concepts offered a way in Christendom for ecclesial and civil authority to mutually support one another and preserve the religious and political institutions of power is not of immediate concern here. The conservative effect of a privatized notion of sin which renders any criticism of civil authority an immoral act and any criticism of ecclesial power a crime is treated adequately elsewhere.[7]

What is of interest here is that such a context of mutually supportive systems of civil and religious authority and power would clearly prefer notions of sin which defined this reality as an act of rebellion by which an individual transgressed one of the laws of God, church or state. In such a political and religious situation it is hardly surprising that the mystery of sin would come to be identified with the transgression of a law and the experience of the sinner would be described as an individual lawbreaker. Crime became the primary analogy of human sinfulness, while the sinner was understood primarily as a criminal.[8]

It should be obvious that such a grasp of sin would turn a deaf ear and a blind eye to structural injustices within the systems of (ecclesial or civil) law and order. The crime model presumes the innocence or rightness of the legal structures, defining injustice or violence solely in terms of rebellion.

Tendency Toward Legalism

One of the other contributing factors leading to the centrality of the crime model in certain epochs of Christian and

Jewish history has been the tendency of religious ethics to lose touch with an original and more relational grasp of morality and to shift toward a more rigorous and often rigid legalism. This tendency to focus on external observance of the law over personal or communal conversion is evident in the shift from the classical prophets to post-exilic Judaism's focus on strict observance of the letter of the law.[9] The notion of covenant is understood in a more extrinsic and juridical sense. This is also seen in the development of canon law in Roman Catholicism, especially in the influence this new field of study had upon Catholic morality and sacramental theology.

In moral theology the influence of canon law helped to generate an increasingly casuistic and legalistic perspective, while in sacramental theology the same influence focused more and more attention on the minimal conditions of liceity and validity. In seminaries much of the theology in these areas was taught and understood from a legalistic perspective. This tendency only accentuated a reliance upon juridical and individualistic categories in moral theology's treatment of sin by framing the theological questions regarding confession in juridical language. In fact, the whole of moral theology, confined to an act-analysis of the sins of individuals, was perceived by many to be the partner or stepchild of canon law.[10]

Penance: The Practical Issue

The major determinant, however, to the course moral theology has taken in the treatment of sin has been the practice of private confession initiated by Celtic monks in the sixth century. No other single factor has played such a crucial role in the embedding of juridical and individualistic models of sin in the Catholic consciousness.[11]

To begin with, this very structure of this "private" sacrament of penance invites the sinner, confessor and believing community to envision sin primarily, if not exclusively, in personal and individual categories.[12] To the degree that this sacrament was perceived by many, if not most, Catholics to be the ordinary means of experiencing sacramental forgiveness was it logical to conceive of sin in a private framework? The sin to be confessed in the confessional box was the free and intentional transgression of a divine or ecclesial law by an *individual*. Personal sins, crimes against God, were "real" sins. Any other understanding was peripheral and analogous.

Secondly, the way in which the sacrament was "celebrated" (a relatively recent term for the penitent's experience of what occurred in confession) significantly contributed to the use of juridical and legalistic models. The penitent came before the priest-confessor, listing according to species and number the sin-crimes committed since his last confession. The confessor, listening as a judge to these self-accusations, would then ascertain the severity (misdemeanor, felony, capital offense) of the sins catalogued, assign a penance appropriate to the crimes and pardon the sinner. In this way the priest performed the three basic functions of a jurist confronted with a criminal. It is therefore not surprising that the Council of Trent understood confession and absolution in juridical categories.[13]

The real significance of penance's influence upon moral theology, however, is perhaps most clearly seen in the dual traditions of the penitentials and the manuals. Both of these collections were prepared with the intention of offering very practical guides which might assist the priest-confessor fulfill one of his basic juridical roles in the sacrament of penance:

(1) that of determining culpability (judging), and/or (2) that of assigning a penance (punishing).

The penitentials, lists compiled for an itinerant and uneducated clergy, sought to offer a systematic, and therefore just, approach to the assignment of penances. As Häring notes,

> These penitentials appeared first in Ireland, then in Germany and France. They were composed to aid and direct the confessors in determining the character and degree of sacramental penance he was to impose upon his penitent. Since nothing was to be left to the discretion of the particular confessor, the various species of mortal sin were examined in the most minute detail.[14]

Sinners were, therefore, assigned penances based upon the gravity and type of their sins. These texts, which were hardly works of systematic theology, nevertheless had profound theological import in that they contributed to a primacy of juridical models in the understanding of sin and forgiveness.[15]

The manualist tradition, on the other hand, emphasized the juridical task of ascertaining culpability. The manuals of moral theology, written for clergy responsible for the moral guidance of the faithful, particularly in the sacrament of confession, provided an in-depth analysis of personal culpability, discussing several factors which might either mitigate or contribute to the guilt of the sinner. With the aid of an education in moral theology provided by the manuals, the confessor was to ascertain whether a sin had been committed, if the penitent was subjectively culpable, and what was the degree of that culpability. Such inquiries and distinctions were completely consistent with and supportive of a juridical understanding of the sacrament and the notion of sin.[16]

An Unsuitable Model

As a result of these various factors the mystery of human sinfulness came to be understood primarily in juridical and individualistic categories. The analogy which dominated Catholic morality was that of sin as an act committed by a free and competent individual who violated some law of God, church or state.[17] Sin was a crime. And the sinner was the relatively isolated and therefore free individual who had committed a crime. Employing such juridical and individualistic models rather exclusively, moral theology initiated its task with an analysis of "objective" human acts, abstracted somewhat artificially from the context and story of persons performing them, moved on to an evaluation of the culpability of the identified individual sinner, and brought the process to a conclusion with the assignment of an appropriate penance.

The limits of the juridical and individualistic models of sin are numerous. Among others, the arid legalism and juridicism of traditional moral theology suffers from an alienation from a sound theology of grace, an unawareness of the pervasive and disintegrating power of sin as a state, and an ignorance of the liberating and reconciling God of scripture. Criminal perceptions of sin and sinners tend toward an unreal and Pelagian understanding of human freedom and responsibility, while orienting the person more to punishment than reconciliation. Furthermore, the radical individualism of these models renders moral theology dangerously insensitive to issues of social injustice and uncritical of law-making institutions. The continued reliance upon such models supports a privatized and legalized morality alienated from dogma, scripture and the wealth of human experience and supportive of oppressive systems of power and authority.

The Violence of Innocence

Perhaps one of the most pervasive scandals of the religious experience, transcending every congregational and denominational boundary, is the violence of the innocent. More frightening a question than why God allows evil to happen to good people is why God allows the so-called good people to be so violent to sinners. The scandal of the wrath of the righteous is a terrifying, yet profoundly human (or inhuman) reality. The core of this violence of the innocent against the guilty is revealed in the tendency of the crime model to select separate individuals to serve as a scapegoat for the experience of moral evil in the community, indeed in all persons.

For the violence experienced in the juridical model of sin does not consist simply or finally in certain disproportionate penalties assigned in Catholic morality for what seem today to be relatively minor sins. That Catholics believed a youth could, in the normal course of events, merit eternal damnation for intentionally missing mass on *one* Sunday or for a single act of masturbation is but a symptom of a deeper and more pervasive disorder—the drive to be innocent, achieved through the condemnation of the guilty.

And it is the radical and unchecked individualism of this model which leads to perceptions of sin as a crime and the sinner as a criminal and which therefore isolate the "guilty" party from the human community in a rather artificial manner. The crime model assumes that the sinner is different, even separate, from the rest of humanity. It tends to deny the bibical data that all are sinners. Furthermore, the ambiguity of the experience of human evil is ignored or denied and a select group of persons is identified as the exclusive cause of sin, judged guilty and (quite logically) sentenced to punishment. In this way the larger group and the majority of its members are able to maintain a sort of pseudo- or taboo innocence.

Thus, criminal models of sin cooperate in a disassociative process by which the community of the "innocent" project the shared experience of moral and religious evil onto the "guilty." Such a procedure is intrinsically immoral, radically violent and profoundly un-Christian.[18]

The violence of this model seems even more glaring when contrasted with the response of Jesus to such moral juridicism. The gospels continuously report on his reaction to the self-righteous who disdained contact with the unclean and judged sinners without mercy or compassion, thanking God that they were not like other men. The scandal of Jesus' dining with tax collectors, having his feet bathed by a prostitute and asking an adulterous Samaritan woman for a cup of water constantly provoked the wrath of the "innocent." The scandal of Jesus was his forgiveness, his commitment to reconcile sinners and his undying gift of redemptive and transforming love. The one who did not come to judge but to give life did not deem his innocence or untouchability something to be grasped at, but embraced persons while they were still sinners. Unlike the innocence of some of the Pharisees, which placed heavy burdens of guilt on others without lifting one finger to help the sinner, the innocence of Jesus was such that "he who knew not sin became sin for our sake." In such a light the concept of sin as crime and sinner as criminal seems an abandonment of the gospel vision.[19]

A Blind Eye

The problem here is somewhat ironic. While many are arguing for a renewed sense of sin, it may well be that traditional models served the function of relieving large segments of the human community of any real sense of responsibility for the presence of sin in the world. By projecting the experience of such sinfulness rather exclusively upon a relatively small band of "criminals," these models cooperated with a disassociative process in which there was, despite all the fire and brimstone, not a very strong sense of sin at all. As Jesus warned his contemporaries, the fixation upon this small speck of individual sins in others has rendered them/us blind to the rather large plank of human sinfulness present in themselves. Tragically, this use of criminal language would have the same disintegrating effect on the intra-psychic level, as is obvious from the psychological research upon the disassociative power of shame and guilt.[20]

The Free and Individual Sinner

One of the reasons for this violent tendency in juridical models of sin is that such models tend to presume an unrealistic degree of freedom in the agent. By initiating its analysis with the examination of the "objective" structure of the act, moral theology has allowed considerations of the context, story and character of the person to be relegated to a secondary position. Thus, while factors mitigating individual freedom (impediments) have traditionally played a role in moral analysis, contemporary theologians have argued that the grasp of the contextualization of personal freedom by biological, psychological and social factors was rather shallow. Earlier moral theology seemed to argue for the existence of a personal freedom essentially unaffected by the conditional and peripheral contexts which constituted the impediments to that freedom's exercise. The insights of biology, depth and social psychology and sociology reveal the inadequacy of that position and the anthropology upon which it was based.[21]

The grasp of personal freedom evident in both traditional moral theology's employment of juridical models and civil society's subscription to what Gerald McHugh has referred to as "penal ideology" is both incomplete and uncontextualized.[22] There is no serious attempt to understand either the way in which categorical freedom of choice is radically situated by the context, story or limits of the reacting person or the manner in which the power of sin pervades the totality of personal experience and frustrates that freedom (transcendental) which struggles to integrate one's life.

Instead, the criminal model assumes that the origin and experience of sin can be rather completely encapsulated within the free will of the individual agent, a free will more or less independent of mitigating factors or impediments except in a peripheral sense. According to this highly individualistic anthropology, sinful behavior is simply the expression of a rebellious will transgressing the laws of God. Since the will is the origin and font of sinful reality, the individual person is to be held not only responsible but criminally culpable for all sins, and the will is to be broken or re-educated through punishments.[23]

By so radically sundering the person from the context of community the criminal model develops an uncontextualized and narrow grasp of both human freedom and responsibility. Freedom is perceived primarily within the framework of isolated categorical choices made by a solitary person. In such a light responsibility is reduced to the accountability for sinful actions which the person experiences *as an individual.* There is no attempt to come to grips with the broader experiences of human freedom or responsibility. Criminal models are concerned only with a rather uncontextualized grasp of individual freedom and culpability.

Lacking Compassion

Needless to say, such a model is profoundly lacking in either compassion for the sinner or any orientation toward forgiveness. Nor is this coincidental. For there are some basic assumptions present in this model which put it in conflict with a gospel understanding of either the call to compassion or the need for forgiveness for the sinner. They are:

1. that the person sins only as an individual,
2. that the sinning individual is different from others, particularly in his/her "willfulness,"
3. that this "willfulness" needs to be broken or punished,
4. that the crime of sin needs to be expiated through a penalty which will return us to the original state of justice.

Such an understanding of the sinner tends to be devoid of any recognition of the common humanity of all sinners, the weakness, frailty and sinfulness of all persons, the need all persons have of forgiveness, and the gospel call of Christ to reach out in compassion and forgiveness to the sinner. Instead, because the focus of the crime model is upon the sinner as individual, ignoring his/her connection to the freedom, history, and sins of all other persons and indeed of the human community, it tends to scapegoat these same individual sinners as carriers of the guilt of the community. It can do this primarily because it asserts or at least implies that the sinner is separate from and unlike the rest of humanity, that he/she is different, and thus to be treated differently, less humanely.

Furthermore, the crime model tends to have a distorted perception not only of the sinner, but of his/her exercise of human freedom. For the model focuses on freedom only from the perspective of obedience to the law. In this context the exercise of freedom is understood as a "willful" or malicious character of the person. Sinfulness is willfulness, pride, arrogance, while holiness is docility, obedience, meekness. This understanding of freedom is not unlike the hospital staff that describes a "good" patient as one who never bothers them, or the parents who describe a "perfect" baby as one that never cries. There is little or no notion of the creative, even divine character of human freedom. For the law sees freedom primarily as the capacity to stray, to err, to rebel. And the response to this freedom-as-a-threat is enforcement or punishment.[24]

Given this unnuanced grasp of human freedom as profoundly individual and radically unchecked and the sinner as particularly "willful," it is not too surprising that this model also tends to assume that human sinfulness can be rather easily vanquished. The sinner/criminal could easily enough turn from sin if he/she were properly motivated. The long-term employment and drastic failure of the crime model and its assumptions of willful prisoners in our penal system makes it obvious that this is not the case, and that persons, especially the criminal sinners, are not nearly so free or so "willful" as the model assumes. Sin is not so easily dismissed or disposed of by the act of will of the sinner. Paul made this point more than clear to us, as have indeed the real and lived experience of billions of sinners since. The crime model is naively cavalier in its assertion that sinners could easily turn their wills from sin, and lack only the proper motivation. The sinner is not nearly so free.

Lacking Forgiveness

The failure to focus on forgiveness is not only a result of the model's inability to recognize the common humanity of all sinners, though this is a large and dangerous part of the problem. The crime model is grounded in a particular worldview which understands reality as a divinely ordered and sanctioned status quo. Justice consists in the preservation of the balance of this order, while injustice and violence consist in upsetting this balance. This concept of justice and world order is not biblical, but Greek. Such a worldview is interested in punishing the individual sinner in order to re-establish an original order of justice. It thus tends to assume the need for punishing the disobedient individual, while being (as previously noted) blind to the possible guilt of the community or the presence of injustice or violence in the very structures of the status quo. Such justice is primarily concerned with the maintenance of "law and (especially) order."

The crime model relies upon the presumption that the present order is innocent, even more than innocent, righteous. This righteous order represents the divinely-sanctioned structure of reality which is violated by sin, and which must be defended by an equal and opposite act of violence, restoring the original order.

According to this model, sins are violations of the divinely sanctioned order, violations which scream out for a punishment that will restore the original order and thus expiate the offense committed by the sinner. In this model crime must lead to punishment, otherwise there can be no real expiation of the imbalance introduced into the system. Forgiveness is a sign of chaos, of weakness, but not of virtue. Forgiveness has no real place or reasonable meaning in this worldview. Punishment is the measure of the justice of a system. Crime demands it.

It is obvious that such a grasp of divine justice is not consistent with either the God who rescued, forgave and redeemed the Israelites or the Son of God who died on the cross to save the sinners, not the righteous. The justice of the God of the Hebrews and of Jesus the Christ is liberating, redemptive, transformative, salvific and forgiving. The justice of God is merciful and compassionate. The assumptions of the crime model are inconsistent with this grasp of reality. For according to the biblical worldview, sins do not cry out for expiation as much as sinners cry out for forgiveness.

Conclusion

From all of this it seems obvious that the crime model suffers from serious defects as a way of understanding the reality of the mystery of human sinfulness. Such a model tends toward punitive scapegoating of the powerless, turning a blind eye to profounder and more pervasive experiences of sin. It also tends to be based on a rather Pelagian anthropology, which reflects a poorly developed grasp of human freedom. The overriding characteristics of individualism and juridicism render this model inadequate to serve as the basis of a Christian theology of sin.

Notes

1. Rondet, *The Theology of Sin,* 83.

2. Gerald McHugh, *Christian Faith and Criminal Justice* (New York: Paulist Press, 1978) 166f.

3. David Hollenbach, *Claims in Conflict: Retrieving the Catholic Human Rights Traditions* (New York: Paulist Press, 1979) 13–20.

4. The role of western individualism, especially in contributing to the juridical categories of thought in Catholic moral theology, is discussed in, among others, Norbert Rigali "Sin in a Relational World," *Chicago Studies* 23:3 (1984) 321–323; Agnes Cunningham, SSCM, "The Greek Fathers: An Alternative to Augustine," *Chicago Studies,* 21:3 (1982) 239–253; Eugene Cooper, "The Notion of Sin in Light of the Theory of the Fundamental Option—The Fundamental Option Revisited," *Louvain Studies,* 9:4 (1983) 376; Curran, *Themes in Fundamental Moral Theology,* 148.

5. Leo XIII is shown to give backing to this position in Donal Dorr, *Option for the Poor* (Maryknoll: Orbis, 1983) 29–51.

6. Emil Brunner, *Justice and the Social Order* (New York: Harper & Row, 1945) 118.

7. While political and liberation theologians highlight the conservative effect of a privatized grasp of morality, serving the needs of the oppressors, a keen insight into individual guilt's function is provided in Jean Remy, "Fault and Guilt in

the Perspective of Sociology," *Concilium,* 61: Dogma (New York: Herder and Herder, 1971) 10–25.

8. Excellent discussions of the relation between sin and crime are to be found in Menninger, *Whatever Became of Sin?* 50–73; McHugh, *Christian Faith and Criminal Justice,* 11–31.

9. Coventry, "Sixteenth and Twentieth Century Concepts of Sin," 51. Maly, *Sin: Biblical Perspectives,* 2.

10. Thomas Slater, S.J., *A Short History of Moral Theology* (New York: Benziger Brothers, 1909) 20–22; McHugh, *Christian Faith and Criminal Justice,* Häring, 21–24; *The Law of Christ,* vol. 1; O'Connell, *Principles for a Catholic Morality,* 17.

11. Gaffney, *Sin Reconsidered,* 6; Rigali, "Sin in a Relational World," 328–330; Cooper, "Notion of Sin in Light of Fundamental Option," 380; Robert Hater, "Sin and Reconciliation: Changing Attitudes in the Catholic Church," *Worship,* 59:1 (1985) 19–20; Peter Henriot, "The Concept of Social Sin," *Source Book on Poverty, Development and Justice,* Education Staff of the Campaign for Human Development, eds. (Washington, D.C.: U.S. Catholic Conference, 1973) 68; Gregory Baum, *Religion and Alienation* (New York: Paulist Press, 1975) 198; Patrick Kerans, *Sinful Social Structures* (New York: Paulist Press, 1974) 57–59; Bernard Häring, *The Law of Christ,* vol. 1 (Westminster: Newman Press, 1961) 10–22; Henri Rondet, S.J., *The Theology of Sin* (Notre Dame: Fides, 1960) 45–49, 65–71; Christian Duquoc, "Real Reconciliation and Sacramental Reconciliation," *Concilium,* 61: Dogma (New York: Herder and Herder, 1971) 26–37.

12. Monden, *Sin, Liberty and Law,* 44; Franz Nikolasch, "The Sacrament of Penance: Learning from the East," *Concilium,* 61: Dogma (New York: Herder and Herder, 1971) 67.

13. Mondon, *Sin, Liberty and Law*, 44.

14. Häring, *Law of Christ*, 10.

15. O'Connell, *Principles for a Catholic Morality*, 12–13.

16. Häring, *Law of Christ*, 18–20; O'Connell, *Principles for a Catholic Morality*, 18.

17. Timothy O'Connell, "A Theology of Sin," *Chicago Studies 21:3 (1982)* 282.

18. Relevant discussions of "innocence" and "criminals" can be found in Rollo May, *Power and Innocence: A Search for the Source of Violence* (New York: W. W. Norton and Co., 1972) 47–64; Karl Menninger, *The Crime of Punishment* (New York: The Viking Press, 1966); McHugh, *Christian Faith and Criminal Justice*, 100–104; Monden, *Sin, Liberty and Law*, 154–156.

19. Monden, *Sin, Liberty and Law*, 156; Rondet *The Theology of Sin*, 26.

20. Norbert Schiffers, "Guilt and Moral Evil in Light of the Study of Behavior," *Concilium*, 56: Moral Theology (New York: Herder and Herder, 1971) 58; Henri Niel, "The Limits of Responsibility," in *Sin*, trans. Bernard Murchland, C.S.C. (New York: Macmillan, 1962) 48; Marc Oraison, Psychology and the Sense of Sin," in *Sin*, 32.

21. Monden, *Sin, Liberty and Law*, 19–43; Niel, "The Limits of Responsibility," 53–54. Piet Schoonenberg, S.J., *Man and Sin: A Theological View* (Notre Dame: University of Notre Dame Press, 1965) 105.

22. McHugh, *Christian Faith and Criminal Justice*, 86–129.

23. *Ibid.*, 166–183; Menninger, *The Crime of Punishment*, 16–27.

24. McHugh, *Christian Faith and Criminal Justice*, 166–169.

5
∎

SIN AS PERSONAL

∎ ∎ ∎

Introduction

In our discussion of the crime model we noted that sin
∎ was normally defined as "actual" referring to the fact
that sin was understood as an act or deed violating the laws
of God. But sin is not only "actual," it is also "personal."
That is, sin is not adequately understood simply as a deed
which breaks divine law, but as the personal (free and conscious) choice to contravene such laws. As the NRA might
have phrased it, acts don't sin, persons do. It is impossible to
understand sin without a personal reference point, for the
simple reason that it is impossible to sin without human
agency. Sin does not take place in the vacuum of the laboratory or under simulated conditions in an abstract case discussion. Sin is better understood as the repudiation of the will of
God by a human person.

The "personal" character of sin is revealed in its consequences as well. For sin causes a rift in the relationships and
covenants in which persons find themselves. Sin alienates us
from God and our neighbor. The experience of being a person is radically affected by sin.

It is for these reasons that not only "actual" but also "personal" sin has a long-standing tradition of being employed as a primary model of the mystery of human sinfulness. For the "personal" dimension underscores two central elements of the traditional understanding of sin: the (a) agency and (b) alienating consequences of sin. Not only must the deed be done, but the sinful deed must be the expression of a personal subject who finds himself/herself in an interpersonal context. Otherwise the notion of responsibility has no real meaning.

1. A TURN TO THE PERSON

Personal Sin and a Personal God

From Act to Person. With Vatican II the church called for a reform of moral theology. In the main part this reform was in response to a growing consensus that the discipline had lost contact with the life-giving fonts of scripture and dogmatic theology, coming more and more under the shadow of canon law. This disconnection had led to a Catholic morality characterized by strong tendencies of legalism, minimalism, and an arid casuistry dominated by act-analysis and leading to rigidly juridical and severely punitive measures in response to the sinner. The council documents called for a move away from this extrinsicist and legalistic morality and a shift toward an ethic focused on the personal relationship between God and humanity.

In many ways the developments brought about by this reform movement constituted significant improvements over the previous state of affairs. Three very significant shifts characterized the move to a more personalistic grasp of morality in general and human sinfulness in particular.[1]

Away from Legalism. In the personalist understanding of sin law ceased to serve as the primary model of the relation between the human and divine. This meant that morality need not be characterized by legalism or minimalism. In its place theologians wrote in personalistic language about a covenantal bond uniting God and humans, or about morality in the context of a personal vocation to discipleship. The dynamic and personal character of morality came to the forefront.

Away from Brimstone. As a result of this shift from legalism to personalism morality was understood in less juridical and punitive terms. The harshness and severity of numerous penalties seemed inconsistent with a renewed sense of a loving and personal God. What might have been tolerable behavior in the almighty lawgiver and judge seemed out of character in the one who had given his only beloved to die on a cross.

Away from Act-Analysis. Another major development occurred in the move beyond both an exclusive reliance upon act-analysis and a strong tendency toward an overly abstract casuistry in moral theology. Catholic moralists, employing the insights of the social sciences, focused more and more attention not on the objective structure of the material act, but on the intentionality of the personal agent. While intentionality had always been a constitutive element of moral analysis, contemporary reflections stepped beyond and behind human intentionality as it referred to categorical decisions and sought to discover the moral meaning of the human person standing behind all his/her decisions. In this framework the sinful deed or act was perceived as an expression of a decision to repudiate one's own vocation at the core or heart of the human person. This would be the understanding of sin as mortal. Indeed, this was the fullest understanding of sin as personal.

From Person to Person. At the same time these various shifts highlighted not only the personal nature of the sinful agent but also the profoundly interpersonal character of the sinful choice. Sin was not only an expression of the malice of the agent, but also constituted an offense against a personal God and (normally) rendered some harm to the covenantal neighbor. By describing the personal context as relational, employing terms like "vocation" and "covenant," sin was seen as a repudiation of a personal God's invitation to live in community with others. This interpersonal dimension moved beyond the focus on the malice of the personal subject to the harm rendered the object of one's sin. Thus the wrongness of sin, in this personal model, was not located in the violation of an extrinsic law. Instead, it was found in both the *malice* of the personal (free and conscious) sinner and the *harm* rendered to another personal subject or subjects. In this sense "personal" sin referred not only to the subject or agent, but also to the object or recipient of the harm. Sin becomes personal by being interpersonal.

This emphasis was in part a recovery of the biblical notion of sin as "alienation," an image which captured the disordering reality and effects of sin in terms of one's relationships. Here the sinner was not simply one who had broken the law, but one who stood alienated in hostile chaos, at odds with God, neighbor, creation and the self. Indeed, the depth and breadth of this notion reached beyond the western perspective of the individual person and his/her relationships, including communal, societal, ecological and cosmic dimensions too often forgotten in the focus on the person. In this way the full scope of sin as alienation was not (as we shall see) given enough attention.[2]

As a result of these developments moral theology corrected a number of the excesses and moved beyond certain of the most severe limits of the earlier juridical vision of morality. The shift from legalism to personalism constituted a real improvement in the state of moral theology and offered a richer and more accurate grasp of the mystery of human sinfulness, especially of the notions of personal malice and interpersonal harm.[3]

Personal Sin and Personalism

The theological vision of the council was, however, not the only root of the growing concern for and turn to the personal. Nor was dissatisfaction with the legalism of moral theology the only reason for theologians or others to stress the import and the role of the personal subject. Instead, the turn to the personal subject could point to a number of causes, theological and cultural, historical and contemporary.

Individualism. Within the west, especially since the Enlightenment, the import of the individual person had been a constant focus. This long-standing tendency toward sometimes radical individualism found a growing ally in both the Enlightenment's increasing focus upon the liberation of the individual and liberal democracy's stress upon the political rights and liberties of individual persons. The burgeoning importance given to the defense of personal rights and liberties in the latter half of this century has further enhanced the stress upon the personal.

Anti-Institutionalism. The individualism of the west found another ally in the growing unease developing in the latter part of this century with both the collectivist and totalitarian societies on the one hand and an increasingly technological and specialized global community on the other. In the face of both of these phenomena there has been an increasing stress upon the dignity, rights and import of the human person. The shift to the person here has been an act of defense, drawing a line against the encroaching domination of the collective or whole. Personalism has served as a banner waved from the embattlements, defending the rights of the individual. This trend is evidenced in the political realm in the discussion of personal rights and in the philosophical world by the growth of existentialism.

Right to Privacy. When the Supreme Court discovered this right in *Roe vs. Wade,* it defined a rather absolute boundary between the so-called public realm of law and private sphere of morality. This separation is often articulated in the unnuanced adage that "you can't legislate morality," usually meant to suggest that law has nothing to do with the private sphere of morals. Instead, morality is understood as having to do primarily with matters of sexual behavior or religious practice, while the law is concerned with the public commerce of persons in society. This radical separation of the two realms meant that sin was rendered a purely private matter, addressing only issues of personal concern over which civil authority had no jurisdiction. Sin was personal, crime was public, and ne'er the twain shall meet.

According to this dualistic vision of reality the appropriate place for the religious or moral voice is in the area of private affairs, such as sexual ethics or religious beliefs. Sin can only be spoken about meaningfully within these categories, and thus the religious community has neither the authority nor the competence to cry out against societal ills or injustices. One hears this response often enough from ruffled congregations unhappy with their ministers' excursions into the social realm.

When the reforms which had been called for by the council are contextualized within these other forces we note that the shift from legalism to personalism in moral theology tended to have the unintended side-effect of limiting sin to the realm of the personal or interpersonal as opposed to the communal or social.[4] In other words, the shift from act-analysis did overcome the juridical character but not the radical individualism of Catholic morality.[5] Personal sin became private sin.

This is an extremely significant point, for it means that the reform of moral theology is but half done. The move beyond legalism is insufficient unless it is accompanied by a critique of the dominance that individualistic categories have in Catholic moral thought. As long as one's "personal" relation to the divine is understood as meaning "private," the covenantal grasp of grace and sin has been artificially squeezed into exclusively personalistic categories. Sin has been privatized.

Personal Sin Becomes Private Sin

As a result of a number of these factors we are confronted with several ways of understanding human sinfulness as personal. Some are helpful, others are not. Sin is clearly personal in the sense that it involves a personal, that is, free and conscious choice, on either the categorical or the transcendental level. Sin is personal in that sin is the expression of a human subject, either in a peripheral and somewhat less serious decision, or in a fundamental and mortal repudiation of God's grace. Furthermore, the personal character of sin is also revealed in its intersubjective and relational context and meaning. In other words, personal sin refers to the personal agency and personal subject of sin, as well as its interpersonal effects. Thus, "personal" sin underscores the malice and the harm of sin, an expression of disordering freedom.

Discussions, however, of "personal" sin which fail to take note of the profoundly individualistic tendencies of much of Western, rational, analytical, existential or "personalistic" thought tend to support of juxtaposition of "personal" and "social" sin, which sees the former as both private and more real. In this way is sin radically privatized. Religious and moral authority is delimited to the realm of the personal, and the only sin which is real is that which is consciously and freely done by one individual to another with the intent to do harm. Sin, in this understanding, seems to cover little more than interpersonal unkindness.

There is a certain tragedy here. Although the shift beyond legalism was an advance, the move to personalism has in some ways so narrowed and focused the understanding of sin that morality becomes obsessed with the intentionality and self-understanding of the individual. This is hardly a sufficient vantage point from which to be doing moral theology.[6]

2. SIN BEYOND PERSONAL SIN

A Criticism of Private Sin

This individualistic grasp of human sinfulness has recently come under serious criticism from a number of voices in various branches of the sacred and social sciences and from those reflecting upon the lived experience of the mystery of sin. The alienating power and destructive state of human sinfulness is not explainable within the narrow parameters of individualism.

Indeed many have argued that the continuing failure of the sacrament of reconciliation to speak effectively to large segments of the Catholic population is at least partially due to the privatized structure of the sacrament. Such a structure fails to offer a viable way of addressing the lived experience of sin—that is, sin in a communal context.[7]

Sin is not experienced simply or primarily in an individualistic framework. Rather, the mystery of human sinfulness makes its presence felt in the interpersonal, familial, societal, national, ecclesial and global communities of humanity. To paraphrase the gospels, "wherever two or three (or two or three million) are not gathered together, there is sin." The experiences of sin are alienation, oppression, hostility, isolation, manipulation, dependence, inequality, injustice, indifference and violence. They are the experiences of disordered and disintegrating relationships and communities.[8] Thus it is quite appropriate and realistic to speak about sin with such language as "solidarity in sin," "sin-of-the-world," and "sinful social structure" or "social sin."

Biblical Reflections

Biblical theology offers two major insights in the criticism of a privatized notion of sin: (1) the development of a concept of personal accountability deeply embedded within a covenantal context of responsibility, and (2) the perception of the mystery of sin not only (or primarily) as act but as power and state. Both of these insights contribute to a fuller grasp of the mystery of human sinfulness.

Covenantal Responsibility. Biblical scholars agree that the original perception of sin in the Old Testament was on the covenantal or community level.[9] Sin was the alienation of God and the community of the chosen people experienced through punitive measures responding to violations of the covenantal taboos. This primitive corporate grasp of sin was dominated by a magical and somewhat pre-ethical model which understood sin as a "missing of the mark" or error (not necessarily moral) for which the entire people might be punished. Neither intentionality nor personal responsibility seemed a relevant issue.[10] Individual ancestors, kings or prophets who "sinned" did so primarily as representatives of Israel in its relationships to God.

With the growth of covenantal theology notions of intentionality and personal responsibility came more to the fore, being most clearly developed in the writings of Jeremiah (31:29) and Ezekiel (ch. 18). Here the notions of personal culpability and individual responsibility for sins committed against the covenant were firmly established.[11] At the same time work among other prophetic voices such as Isaiah and Amos took the notion of sin beyond taboo and magic into the ethical realm of personal and interpersonal relationships.

However, while the introduction of personal responsibility and individual accountability represented a major development over the primitive taboo mentality which preceded it, it is not obvious that this move constitutes an abandonment of covenantal notion of sin. Some tendencies toward legalism in post-exilic Judaism tended to support a privatized grasp of sin and morality but it would be erroneous to understand such a trend as more authentic than the social message of the classical prophets or the gospels. Within these central strains of biblical thought there is a strong sense of corporate or covenantal sinfulness, dominated not by categories of magic or taboo, but by a profound sense of injustice and alienated relationships. The classical prophets and the gospels are aware of sin on the personal *and* covenantal levels, not as competitive or mutually exclusive but as interconnected and mutually interrelated. The best elements of a biblical theology employ a variety of models and categories to speak about the multiple ways in which the mystery of sin is experienced. It would be inaccurate to contend that a privatized notion of personal sin has any sort of primacy in a hierarchy of biblical models.[12] Instead, a covenantal notion of sin as alienation experienced in the multiple relations (interpersonal, corporate, ecological) of life seems to more adequately express this radical experience of humanity's disordered relation to God. Biblical theology does not support an individualistic notion of sin.

Sin as Power and State. The biblical perception of sin as more than individual rebelliousness is further evidenced in the employment of the two models of sin as power and state. New Testament theology especially speaks of sin not merely or primarily as the free choices of individuals to transgress the laws of God. By speaking of sin in the singular, Pauline and Johannine theology step behind the separate experiences of particular "sins" to the mysterious ground from which they spring, i.e. SIN.[13]

Paul's attempts to wrestle with temptations which continuously mocked and defeated the best efforts of his free will called him to an awareness of a power of sin which transcends and contextualizes individual liberty. His understanding of the malice of a "flesh" turned against and hostile to the "spirit," far from being an expression of Cartesian or Gnostic dualism, speaks of an awareness of a power within and over the very core of the person, a power which frustrates the struggle of the spirit to integrate and make whole the human experience.[14]

John's grasp of a "world" hostile to the mission of Jesus and the preaching of the gospel reveals an understanding of sin as a pervasive and corruptive state inimical to the work of repentance and conversion. The "world" is not simply the natural order of reality distinguished from the supernatural kingdom of God, but the experience of a creation and humanity disordered from itself and its ground by the experience of sin, an experience which has poisoned the whole breadth of human experience.[15]

Stepping beyond the language of "flesh" and "world," the theological efforts of these authors reflect an awareness of the mystery of sin which transcends individualism and embraces the communal character of this experience. The discussion of SIN in the singular instead of singular sins underscores this Pauline and Johannine insight.

Dogmatic Reflections

Dogmatic theology raises serious questions about a privatized grasp of sin or morality when it develops an integral notion of God's graciousness. Contemporary discussions of the relational character of grace as a sharing in the life of the Trinity, along with a resurgence of an appreciation of the role of the community in sacramental experiences of grace, suggest a perception of God's graciousness which transcends individualistic categories and speaks of grace as reconciling, healing and forgiving. Such an understanding of grace tends to underscore the perception of sin as alienation, oppression, hostility and injustice, models situating sin in a communal or social category.[16] With a shift away from a

quantitative and toward a relational and even communitarian grasp of grace it seems logical to move beyond a
privatized perception of sin.

"Relational" Sin

In moral theology itself numerous authors have criticized
the inadequacies of an individualistic grasp of sin. Schoonenberg's ground-breaking work on "sin-of-the-world" argued
persuasively for an understanding of human sinfulness which
included but transcended the category of personal sin.[17] Sin
writ large, Schoonenberg argued, precedes, anticipates,
tempts and moves beyond the categories of personal sin. Sin is
more than the quantitative accumulation of individual acts of
sinfulness. It embraces manifestations of malice encoded
within institutional and societal structures, cultural patterns
and political and economic systems. Such sin can hardly be
reduced to individualistic categories.

Echoing Schoonenberg's concerns, Curran and Rigali
have criticized the individualism of traditional Catholic morality.[18] Such individualism ignores the alienating and disintegrating experience of sin on the relationships of the human
person and community, considering such alienation merely
as the peripheral consequences of sinful acts. It also pays too
little heed to the essential social character of the human
person. Curran maintains that sin needs to be understood as
the alienation of fundamental human relations—to God,
other, creation and self. A view which sees sin primarily as
act or transgression pays too little attention to the experience of alienation.[19] Rigali contends that individualistic categories overlook the intrinsic communitarian nature of humanity. Employing personal sin as the primary analogy of

sinfulness blinds Catholic morality to the broader dimensions of a more complete anthropology.[20]

Social Sin

Another voice criticizing the reliance upon individualistic models of sin has been the constantly developing tradition of Catholic teachings on social justice coming from both the magisterium and theologians.

The past century, especially in the last three decades, has witnessed a steadily increasing flow of hierarchical documents dealing with questions of institutional injustices within the political, economic and cultural systems which are intended to render life more humane, just and peaceful.[21] Writings by pontiffs, ecumenical councils, international synods, national conferences and local bishops have abounded on questions of social justice and its relation to the gospel ethic of Jesus. Although the writings have not yet arrived at the mature state of complete synthesis and agreement, and although some of the fundamental notions present in these writings have met with little acceptance within the Catholic community, lay, religious or clerical, it is fair to argue that an overview of this body of material would indicate a high degree of theological consensus supporting the shift away from a primary reliance upon personal and private categories of sin toward a more complete integration of the social and communal aspects of this mystery.[22]

Of particular interest has been the argument of political theologians like Metz and Baum that the privatizing of the gospel message which has characterized the limited vision of western individualism and traditional Catholic morality constitutes an element of social sinfulness.[23] This corporate "blindness," which Jesus criticizes in the Pharisees, is, according to Kerans and Henriot, a part of the western community's sinful resistance to the social message of the gospel.[24]

By limiting the notion of sin to individual deeds of criminal misbehavior, Catholic moral theology has been coopted through silent (and silencing) consent into cooperating with the political and economic systems of power which constitute the status quo. Such a narrow grasp of sin has served the function within the social context of legitimizing the authority of whatever was the current system of governance. In fact this has meant the effective alignment of ecclesial authority *with* the rich and the powerful and (normally) *over* and *against* the poor and the weak.[25] It has also meant the anesthetizing of the oppressors' consciences by defining sinful activity in language of rebellion, law-breaking and criminality, language normally associated with those who are alienated from the reigning political and economic systems or who are interested in the destabilizing of such structures of power. In other words, continued reliance upon privatized notions of sin may well constitute cooperation with sinful systems of oppression and the avoidance or denial of a sense of responsibility of one's ongoing cooperation with such systems. Such cooperation seems clearly sinful.

"Group" Evil

Psychiatry tries to understand the experience of human malice and evil, discover and explain its origins and development and (hopefully) treat and cure its manifestations. Two relatively recent attempts within psychiatry to treat the problem of human malice are to be found in works by Menninger and Peck.[26] What is of particular interest here is that both of these works, while focusing primarily upon the experience of malice in individuals and espousing a real belief in personal responsibility and accountability, have set aside sections for the treatment of group or corporate evil.[27]

In language more commonly associated with social instead of depth psychology each author has attempted to describe the dynamics and destructive patterns of human malice on the corporate level. According to these texts an organization may be characterized by tendencies and behavior patterns which would be considered morally reprehensible if discovered in isolated individuals but which escape the notice or moral outrage of large segments of its population. Such behavior cannot simply be identified with the malice of an individual within the group, no matter how powerful or evil such a person might be. Nor can it be understood as the simple or quantitative accumulation of the malice of individuals. Instead, the group evil seems to be an experience of a cooperative collusion which transcends the normal interpersonal understandings of such cooperation and expresses itself in dynamics reaching beyond the will of any individual or the wills of each taken cumulatively.[28]

And yet there is no suggestion in these texts of an absence of responsibility for this corporate evil. Members of the group experience a contextualized responsibility for the actions and structures of the whole. Indeed, part of the malice of group evil is the tendency to avoid such a sense of responsibility. A great deal of attention is paid in these discussions to tendencies within certain groups to become highly ideological, uncritical of their own self-projections, unwilling to deal openly with internal dissent or external criticism, and violently narcissistic in their relation to other groups.[29] Thus, while underscoring the reality of personal

freedom and responsibility in dealing with evil on the individual or interpersonal level, these authors recognize the limits
of such notions and see the need to incorporate a discussion
of group evil and communal responsibility into their discussion of human malice.

Family Therapy

Another interesting insight into this discussion is provided by psychology in the recent development and growth
of the schools and practice of marriage and family therapy.[30]
Although this burgeoning field consists of a variety of often
competitive approaches and theories, they all seem to share
a common criticism of traditional psychology's individualistic tendencies in the diagnosis and treatment of emotional
illness. Instead of accepting the family's presentation of one
individual member as the so-called "identified patient" or
carrier of psychological illness, these therapists insist on also
examining the structures and patterns of the family system
into which the individual fits.[31]

By employing such a systemic analysis therapy is better
able to understand the origins and functions of the person's
"illness" within the family context and thus better enabled to
offer curative treatment. While not ignoring the reality of
individual illness, responsibility and therapy, marriage and
family counselors insist that a realistic and integral grasp of
emotional illness must understand and treat dysfunctions on
the personal *and* familial level. For example, questions concerning the types of boundaries established and respected
between family members and among the various subsets
within the family grouping, methods and rules of communication among members and success in the acknowledgment,

processing and resolution of conflicts deal with the health of the family and have direct impact upon the wellness of personal members of the family.[32] Furthermore, cycles of transactional games may seriously limit and contextualize the freedom of family members, and it often happens that symptoms of emotional illness in the "identified patient" function as a mask or release valve for serious structural dysfunctions in major task-areas of the family. Individual patterns of neurosis or pathology may be a symptom of, an attempt to deal with or a cover-up for major problems in the family system or one of its subsets.[33]

Again, it is essential to avoid over-simplification. Marriage and family therapists do not deny or ignore the experience of individual illness or therapy. Instead they suggest a view which embraces an awareness of illness on both the individual and the familial level, an awareness recognizing the interrelatedness of these two experiences of illness.[34] Through such an awareness a more integral and realistic grasp of psychological illness and a more effective treatment for its cure is sought.

"Alcoholic Family"

A particular area where the discussion of such illness on the familial level is of interest is to be found in the context of the family of the alcoholic (or any addicted person). Research on the spouses and families of alcoholics has revealed a great deal of truth behind the AA adage that if one lives with an alcoholic for a long enough period there is a strong probability of becoming in many ways as ill as the drinker. Spouses and family members exhibit various sorts of diseased and disintegrating behavior patterns in their relationships with the alcoholic, each other and persons outside the family.[35] Numerous examples of diseased responses are found not only within the various non-drinking members but also in the structures and dynamics of what many have come to refer to as the "alcoholic family" instead of the family of the alcoholic.[36]

Without making any attempt to levy blame or culpability upon the non-drinking members of the alcoholic family or absolve the drinker of all responsibility for his illness or health, research does indicate a certain level of unconscious cooperation in the support of alcoholic behavior. This can be seen in the familial resistance to acceptance of the disease concept or to the recognition of the alcoholic behavior in the blossoming alcoholic. In later stages familial cooperation and deception takes the form of denying the existence of an alcoholic problem through covering up for the alcoholic or moralistically judging the alcoholic for abusive and irrational drinking. Even after the alcoholic has sought treatment and cure in a clinic or program the family members may resent the systematic changes which the recovery and return of a parent figure to the family would imply. The fact that a disproportionate number of widowed spouses enter into second marriages with new alcoholics, and the findings on recent studies of intergenerational effects of alcoholism on children of alcoholics, suggest that language about "alcoholic families" may be more realistic than fanciful.[37]

It is important to note here that this discussion is not about culpability, but responsibility. It is about the ways in which persons with contextualized freedom and limited understanding cooperate in patterns and systems which make evil more present in the world. It is about levels and types of responsibility outside the categories of crime, guilt and punishment, but not outside the realm of real, lived, human experience. To recognize the cooperative effort of numerous

persons in situations of evil is not primarily or always necessarily to assign blame or culpability to some and innocence to
others. Rather, it is to recognize that human responsibility
exists in a variety of forms and on a number of levels. The
alcoholic family, like the alcoholic, does experience a certain
responsibility for the ongoing support of the disease as well
as for the progressive withdrawal of such cooperative support. That is a far cry from saying the disease is their fault, or
that they have the power to cure the alcoholic.

Conclusion

The reforms called for by the council represented an
important step beyond the legalism which had come to dominate moral theology. In this sense the move to the person
constituted an advance. Moral theology was enriched by the
introduction of the dimension of the personal agent, the
personal subject, and the interpersonal context of morality.
So, too, the notion of sin in a "personalist" perspective recap-
tured some of its lost biblical roots and depth.

However, the shift to the personal took place in a context interested in protecting the privacy and rights of the
individual over and against the good of the community. This
sort of polarization tended to understand personal sin as
merely "private," and in this way constituted a real impedi-
ment to the development of a grasp of the societal and communal aspects of sin.

There is no doubt but that sin will always and everywhere be "personal." This does not, however, need to mean
that it will not be social or corporate, nor that such models
are derivative of and secondary to "private" or individual
sin. Indeed, such is clearly not the case.

Notes

1. For an interesting discussion of a "personalist" grasp of sin, cf. Alphonse Spilly, "Sin and Alienation in the Old Testament: The Personalist Approach," *Chicago Studies,* 1982 vol. 21 (3) 211–226.

2. An excellent treatment of this image is developed in Bernard Häring, *Sin in the Secular Age,* Chapter Two: "Sin as Alienation and Sins of Alienation," 28–103.

3. A number of these developments are traced in James E. Hug, S.J., "Social Sin: Cultural Healing," in *Chicago Studies,* vol. 23 (3) 333–352, as well as Kevin F. O'Shea, "The Reality of Sin: A Theological and Pastoral Critique," in *The Mystery of Sin and Forgiveness,* ed. Michael J. Taylor, S. J. (New York: Alba House, 1971) 91–112.

4. For a discussion of the effects of this individualism upon American ethics cf. Robert Bellah *et al., Habits of the Heart* (Los Angeles: University of California Press, 1985).

5. Rigali, "Sin in a Relational World," 323.

6. Several authors have noted the privatizing effects that a shift to personalistic categories has had on moral theology. Curran, Rigali, O'Shea, Hug, and Henriot are but a few. Also of interest is Donal Dorr's *Spirituality and Justice* (Maryknoll: Orbis, 1984) 35–51.

7. Hater, "Sin and Reconciliation," 19–20; Duquoc, "Real Reconciliation and Sacramental Reconciliation," 28, 35f.

8. Curran, *Themes in Fundamental Moral Theology,* 145–151; Spilly, "Sin and Alienation," 217.

9. Coventry, "Sixteenth and Twentieth Century Concepts of Sin," 50; Gaffney, *Sin Reconsidered,* 23; Hater, "Sin and Reconciliation," 23; Kelly, "Aspects of Sin in Today's Theology," 192; LaVerdiere, "The Need for Salvation,"

232; O'Shea, "The Reality of Sin," 92; Schoonenberg, *Man and Sin,* 99.

10. Spilly, "Sin and Alienation in the Old Testament," 212; Bruce Vawter, "Missing the Mark," *The Mystery of Sin and Forgiveness,* ed. Michael Taylor, S.J. (New York: Alba House, 1971) 27.

11. Coventry, "Sixteenth and Twentieth Century Concepts of Sin," 51; Rondet, *The Theology of Sin,* 13; Schoonenberg *Man and Sin,* 102.

12. Maly, *Sin: Biblical Perspectives,* pp. 17–22. Schoonenberg, *Man and Sin,* 99; O'Shea, "The Reality of Sin," 98; Rondet, *The Theology of Sin,* 13; Coventry, "Sixteenth and Twentieth Century Concepts of Sin," 51; LaVerdiere, "The Need for Salvation," 232; Spilly, "Sin and Alienation in the Old Testament," 212–217; Vawter, "Missing the Mark," 24.

13. Coventry, "Sixteenth and Twentieth Century Concepts of Sin," 54; O'Connell, "A Theology of Sin," 280; LaVerdiere, "The Need for Salvation," 233.

14. Rondet, *The Theology of Sin,* 29–35.

15. *Ibid.,* 36–38.

16. LaVerdiere, "The Need for Salvation," 227–230.

17. Schoonenberg, *Man and Sin,* 101.

18. Curran, *Themes in Fundamental Moral Theology,* 145–158; Rigali, "Sin in a Relational World," 321–332.

19. Curran, *Themes in Fundamental Moral Theology,* 145–151.

20. Rigali, "Sin in a Relational World," 324.

21. See the following sources: David O'Brien, Thomas A. Shannon, eds. *Renewing the Earth: Catholic Documents on Peace, Justice and Liberation* (Garden City: Image Books, 1977); Joseph Gremillion, *The Gospel of Peace and Justice* (Maryknoll: Orbis, 1976); National Conference of Catholic Bishops, *Quest for Justice,* eds. J. Brian Benestad, Francis J.

Butler (Washington, D.C.: United States Catholic Conference, 1981); Richard McCormick S.J. and Charles E. Curran, eds., *Readings in Moral Theology*, No. 5: *Official Catholic Social Teaching* (New York: Paulist Press, 1986).

22. Coventry, "Sixteenth and Twentieth Century Concepts of Sin," 52; Rigali, "Sin in a Relational World," 321–324; Henriot, "The Concept of Social Sin," 72.

23. Johannes Metz, "The Church: Social Function in the Light of a 'Political Theology,' " *Concilium* 36: Fundamental Theology (New York: Paulist Press, 1968) 3–5; Baum, *Religion and Alienation*, 196–198.

24. Kerans, *Sinful Social Structures*, 71; Henriot, "The Concept of Social Sin," 74f.

25. Baum, *Religion and Alienation*, 206–214; Peter McVerry, "Sin: The Social, National and International Aspects," *The Way Supplement*, 48 (1983) 44.

26. Menninger, *Whatever Became of Sin?;* Peck, *People of the Lie.*

27. Menninger, *Whatever Became of Sin?* 94–132; Peck, *People of the Lie*, 212–253.

28. Peck, *People of the Lie*, 220–226.

29. Menninger, *Whatever Became of Sin?*, 95–98; Peck, *People of the Lie*, 223–226.

30. William Nichols and Craig A. Everett, *Systematic Family Therapy: An Integrative Approach* (New York: The Guifford Press, 1987) 90–175.

31. Salvador Minuchin, Bruce L. Rosman, Lester Baker, *Psychosomatic Families* (Boston: Harvard University Press, 1978) 23, 51.

32. W. Robert Beavers, *Successful Marriage*, (New York: W. W. Norton and Co., 1985) 30.

33. Minuchin, *Psychosomatic Families*, 32, 46.

34. Beavers, *Successful Marriage*, 29.

35. Clinebell, *Understanding and Counseling the Alcoholic*, 267–269.

36. Robert J. Ackerman, *Children of Alcoholics: A Guidebook for Education, Therapists, and Parents* (Holmes Beach: Learning Publication, 1978) 5.

37. Clinebell, *Understanding and Counseling the Alcoholic*, 278–280.

6
■
■

THE SPIRAL OF SIN:
A SENSE OF THE DRAGON
■   ■   ■

Introduction: Beyond the Criminal Deed

In the crime model of sin we find ourselves dealing
■ with a perception characterized by a profound, even
radical sort of individualism. For the notion of sin as a
criminal transgression focuses its primary, if not exhaus-
tive, attention upon the isolated deed of the individual
agent. Western analytical thought has been directed to the
study of the substance or essence of this deed, paying significantly less attention to what it has usually considered the
separable and secondary realities of consequence or context. This is very clearly revealed by the predominant tendency to act-analysis in the casuistry of much of traditional
work in moral theology. Sin is the deed, the act. Even in
the Baltimore Catechism we note that the language of personal sin is "actual" sin, focusing upon the commission of
the transgression.[1]

This same model has likewise normally tended to focus
its field of vision to include only the individual agent as the
source or font of sin. (This is not denying that the crime
model of personal sin co-existed with an understanding of

original sin, only noting that the notion of sin as transcending the limits of an agent's free will as exercised in an individual deed is not present in what most moral theologians presented as the primary understanding of sin. Original sin was usually presented as an analogous notion of personal sin, which was *real* sin.) Thus, sin was located in the relatively unimpaired and uninfluenced free will of the sinner. The sinner *as an individual* chooses to sin, to rebel, to break the eternal law(s).

Lack of Realism

While we have previously suggested a number of problems with this model and with its radical individualism, it is necessary now to attend to still another rather serious limit to this notion of sin as crime. It lacks realism. In a very real sense the model reflects an understanding of moral evil which does not ring true to human experience as it is lived in the world. While the focus upon an individual action performed in relative freedom by a conscious agent may indeed reflect our initial understandings of the experience of sin, shall we say our first impression, it fails to stand up to or be corroborated by an acquaintance of any duration. It clearly does not reflect the depth of experience and understanding available to anyone who has had a relationship with sin of any length of time.

For the crime model presents us with a diagram, a photograph of human sin. We have, so to speak, a still life of the crime. This may be of real use in the laboratory or the courtroom, but is of limited value to us in other contexts. Such a diagram of sin fails to focus in on the dynamic, historical, even lively (here perhaps the word deadly or pathological would be better) character of sin. Sin as a transgression is too often sin under the slide of a microscope, sin as a specimen, sin in the cage of the local zoo. Such a photograph or still life of sin is helpful in introducing us to the reality of moral evil, or in explaining some of the characteristics of this reality, but it misses the depth dimension of time, of story; and the story of sin is as important as any picture of it might be, perhaps more so.[2]

For indeed our experience of sin over any real length of time reveals a depth character or dimension not noticed in the single individual act. Our acquaintance with sin tends to be repetitive. We find ourselves committing and confessing the same sins over and over again. They take on an habitual character which seems to mock our best and most resolute efforts at change or reformation. The single isolated sin which is washed away in our first confession is not nearly as haunting or daunting as the insidiously repetitive, habitual and increasingly frustrating failures against the gospel which show up again and again as we make an examination of our conscience prior to entering the confessional.[3] Ruefully looking into the mirror of our souls we find that same stupid flaw taunting us with remorse and ridiculing our renewed resolution to overcome this sin.

Sin here is more than a single act, more than an isolated deed we have freely chosen. Sin is experienced as a habit, as some sort of a disorder of the will, as a power or a demon with a will and plan of its own. Such an experience of sin resonates with Paul and John who speak of sin as a power, tenacious and willful, fighting for dominion of our lives. While some may find the use of language about demons and powers too anthropomorphic there is a real sense that our lived experience of sin goes far beyond the dimensions laid out in the photographic image of sin as a crime.

If once a man indulges himself in murder, very soon he comes to think little of robbing; and from robbing he comes next to drinking and sabbath-breaking, and from that to incivility and procrastination. (Thomas De Quincey, Ib Supplementary Papers)

De Quincey's irony points to another dimension of sin which reaches beyond the limits of the crime model—its malignancy. For not only do we experience sin as a series of habitual actions in our lives, a series resisting our efforts to change, but there is also a sense of the pathological character of sin. Sin not only holds us at bay with insidious traps and failings which keep us from overcoming our imperfections, but it has a tendency to unfold, develop, grow in our lives. Like a malignant pathology sin tends to expand and to sink roots into living human organisms. Small, untidy failings often enough grow and flourish, becoming major and destructive forces in our lives. Little choices tend to set the groundwork for more disastrous and malicious decisions. Sin in some way is experienced as a progression into the dark, a conversion to death, a chronic and pathological moral malignancy. Crime as a single transgression of the laws of God fails to express this chronic and pathological dynamism toward death. Instead, the narrative of Genesis 3–11 illustrates this characteristic quite well, as does a haunting passage in Romans (1:18–32) where Paul describes how the malice of the unbelievers multiplies itself and unfolds in a Pandora's box of sins.

Beyond these considerations, the radical individualism of the crime model blinds us to yet another dimension of the lived experience of sin—contagion. For one of the most fundamental parts of our experience of sin in the world is its

noxious, infectious and contaminative character. In a variety
of ways the sins of one person become the catalyst or occasion of the sin of another. Sin not only leads to further and
greater sin in myself, but in some sense my sin creates a
world where others are weakened, distracted, and even
tempted to sin. The sinful experience is in some real way
passed from one generation to another. My sin in some sense
infects the freedom of another and the tenacious and malignant demon becomes a many-headed dragon surfacing in yet
another soul. Often without being consciously or intentionally acted out, the messages of sin are whispered into the
ears of children, and they are taught so very carefully by
their noxious and poisonous environment to hate and to
repeat the sins of their elders.[4] Indeed, it often seems that
"The fathers have eaten unripe grapes, [and] the children's
teeth are set on edge" (Ez 18:2).

   Not only is sin contagious, however. It is, we discover,
also social. We (not only I) cooperate in common strategies,
institutions and games which embody and sanction immoral
actions and behavioral patterns that oppress, alienate and
destroy other human beings. It is this cooperative and social
dimension of sin, so evident in the lived experience of our
national and international institutions and structures, that is
ignored by the concept of sin as crime.

   When all of these diverse insights of habit, malignancy,
contagion and cooperation are drawn together we have a
grasp of sin with much greater depth, breadth and dynamism. In this light perhaps it would be helpful to speak
about sin as a spiral in which the individual actions and
habits of persons are expressions of a viral cancer within
them, a cancer which is communicated not only from person
to person but from generation to generation, sustained by
the ongoing cooperation of various members and groups and

ever deepening and hardening against the will and salvific love of God. Here is a power of sin of infinitely more realism and terror than that tame specimen of crime as the individual transgression of single persons.

The crime model, in its act-analysis and radical individualism, misses these depth dimensions of the experience of human sinfulness, dimensions which are obvious to persons reflecting on their lived experience of sin in the human story and the story of the human community. Its still-life approach and its focus on the separate individual fail to address seriously the etiology and effects of sin. The crime model fails to take seriously the dynamic and malignant power of sin, often assuming that sin can be easily dismissed, or at least failing to come to grips with the tenacity of sin. And it fails to take seriously the transpersonal and social character of human sinfulness.

Sin: From Act to Habit

Thomas Aquinas begins his discussion of sin in the *Summa Theologiae* (1a2ae; q.71) with an analysis of the relationship between virtue and vice. Aquinas has taken this approach in his discussion of sin because:

This general consideration of morality (and sin) is similar to Aristotle's in that it is more concerned with human character and the formation of virtue than with casuistry, which is the moral evaluation of individual human actions. For both Aristotle and St. Thomas virtues and vices determine the actual course human life takes; they are in some sense determinants of human behavior, or principles of human action. From this it is obvious that this part of the *Summa Theologiae* was intended not so much for the education of priests as ministers of the sacrament of penance, but for the formation of theological minds whose interests in morality would be larger than the context of the confessional.[5]

The decision by Thomas to approach the question of sin from a perspective broader than that of casuistry and act-analysis is indicative of a perception he has that human sinfulness cannot be completely defined within the parameters of a transgression or offense against the eternal law. Instead, he moves to the level of virtue or vice where sin is experienced primarily as a habit or a character trait (in the case of sin, a character flaw).[6]

An individual action represents the conscious and free decision of an agent, the exercise of his/her freedom of choice regarding a particular matter at a certain moment in time. Habits, on the other hand, represent a rather more enduring, persistent, even a deeper sort of decision. For with habits we are dealing with not only a decision about a particular action but about a particular way of being. Habits describe decisions and action not on the level of individual acts but on the level of regular patterns of behavior and traits of character. Indeed the habits of a person reveal and express one's basic character, one's identity, on a deeper level. In this way it may be asserted that the habits of a person are more indicative of one's character and identity than single, isolated actions. Habits are, in a real sense, the wellspring of individual actions, and these same actions are symptoms of the basic character of the person.

It should be noted that the relationship between individual actions and habits is reciprocal in the sense that while such actions tend to be expressive of decisions made on the level of habit, these same habits are actualized and deepened (or modified) through conscious and individual deeds.

When considering the question of sin this insight concerning the interrelation between individual actions and habitual behavior has some important implications. For sin as a single transgression of the law must now be located against the backdrop not only of the instantaneous will of the agent, but also as a part and parcel of the deeper and fuller decision (on the level of behavioral patterns or habits) of the person. Sin here describes not simply the concrete action of the person, but the character which constitutes the font of this and many other actions. Sin is understood more as a core decision of the person, expressed in his/her habitual tendency to choose against the call and love of God.

In this light individual actions, while very important, are better understood as symptoms of a deeper and more pervasive decision to turn against the love of God, as symptoms of a more deeply rooted (and harder to reverse) stance against God. The notion of sin as transgression does not adequately express the depth, the strength, or the resistance to change of this experience of sin.[7]

Vice as Enslavement

This insight into sin is not simply academic. Instead, it points to the fact that in sin we are not dealing with an easily vanquished or dismissible flaw in the human experience. Habitual sin refers to the constant and despair-inducing experience of failure in every attempt not to fall this way again. The habitual character of sin is experienced by each of us as

a threatening, frustrating, disintegrating malice which will
not be wiped away and which mocks our best efforts and the
most sustained attempts of our will to eradicate it. There is
nothing amusing or abstract about such an experience. Sin is
no longer a minor or occasional annoyance. It is a disintegrating, malicious, even quasi-personal power which eludes every attempt to destroy it. It is in this sense that Thomas
refers to sin as vice. For vice refers not only to the fact that
the decision to do evil has been made at a deeper level, that
it is a more "hardened" decision, but also to the fact that the
person experiences himself/herself as terribly unfree in the
face of this sin.

Paul describes this dimension of sin as enslaving vice
well in Romans:

> For though the will to do what is good is in me,
> the performance is not, with the result that instead
> of doing the good things that I want to do, I carry
> out the sinful things I do not want. When I act
> against my will, then, it is not my true self doing it,
> but sin which lives in me.
>
> In fact, this seems to be the rule, that every
> single time I want to do good, it is something evil
> that comes to hand. . . . This is what makes me a
> prisoner of that law of sin which lives in my body
> (Rom 7:18–24).

And although Paul knows well of the freedom and the
moral responsibility of human persons, although he often
enough employs understandings of sin as transgressions.
(Rom 5:14; 2:23; 4:15, among others), as acts of disobedience (Rom 5:15; 2 Cor 5:19), and as voluntary failures (1

Tim 6:10; 2 Tim 3:13), he also understands sin as a kind of power which enslaves the struggling sinner, cripples and ridicules his/her will, and rules over the human person.[8]

It is in this sense that Paul has moved beyond transgression to the level (at least) of vice. For habit not only represents a deeper sort of decision on the part of the agent, but it also points to a profound disorder and experience of unfreedom at this level. Unlike the single action which might be washed away or atoned for with relative ease, a vice points to the way in which our sinful decisions and actions on the categorical level are expressions of a fundamental weakness and disorientation in the face of some moral and/or spiritual malice. The various sins we seem to freely choose and do are at the same time expressions of the power of a sin in the face of which we do not seem so free. This is part of Thomas' insight into sin and vice, not only that it is habitual as repetitive, but also that it is an experience of our being enslaved. It is certainly an insight consistent with a Pauline theology of sin.

Franz Böckle has pointed out that the insight of Paul and John, indeed of biblical theology, into a theology of sin is seen in the way in which they step beyond the limits of the notion of individual transgressions and deal with the deeper and more complex experience of human sinfulness, an experience including freedom and unfreedom. For Böckle illustrates their grasp of the interrelation between the notion of sin as act and sin as state or power.

> In this, two ideas are always in competition with each other—on the one hand, the conviction that man is able to decide for himself and is responsible for his own decisions and, on the other, that actual sins are an expression of his subjection to the

power of sin, thus resulting in a solidarity among
sinners, a perceptible connection between guilty
men.[9]

Thus, when we move beyond the photograph of the
crime model and come to see sin from the perspective of
habit and character, much more of its malice and depth is
revealed to us. From this perspective, that of the struggling
sinner who has felt the repeated sting, weight, and power of
sin in his/her life, we can better understand the use of language and models that tend to describe sin not as a transgression or an expression of our own individual will power, but
as an enslaving master from whose dominion our weakened
wills so badly need liberation.

Sin: From Habit to Pathology

Several years ago a well known psychotherapist by the
name of William Glasser wrote a small text entitled *Positive
Addictions*. In the book Glasser, who had done a great deal
of work studying and helping addicted persons, discussed
what he experienced as the difference between what in another time might have been called virtues and vices. In his
opinion certain forms of behavior or "positive addictions"
had the capacity to reverse disintegrative patterns in people's lives, strengthen their personality, help them to cope
better with stress, and move them more and more toward
integration and full actualization of their talents. Vices or
negative addictions, on the other hand, were not only bad
habits, but insatiable and disordering hungers which normally led to the progressive disintegration and death of the
addicted person.[10]

There is perhaps some danger that a cursory reading of Aquinas' approach to sin from the perspective of virtue and vice may miss this dynamic or malignant dimension of this reality. For at first glance we often tend to think of habits only in terms of their repetitive or episodic character and not from the perspective of their finality, which is how Aquinas understood them. That is to say, virtuous or vicious habits represent a decision on the level of character to orient oneself and move toward a final end or goal. They are, therefore, dynamic, and make no sense unless they advance the person toward this end, whether good or evil. We know from our own experience that habits are not only an expression of a decision a person has made in the past concerning a particular value or good. They are also an ongoing decision which the person continually affirms and which serves as the stepping stone to a fuller and deeper decision.

All of this is to say that there is a certain dynamism which is involved in human sinfulness, a dynamism which is not completely expressed when we refer to sin as a stance or a state, but one which is perhaps better grasped by a phrase like "a hardening of the heart." For not only is sin a stance and a decision on the level of character, not only does Paul talk about sin as a powerful master which has reign over the enslaved sinner, but we also find in New Testament literature the concept of sin as something like a malignancy, a cancerous growth, a progressive and rebellious conversion away from the light of Christ.[11]

John captures much of the depth of this notion when he describes the growing violence of the "world" in response to Jesus' proclamation of the word of God. At first indifferent and apathetic to the call to repentance, rather like Herod's unconverted heart before the Baptizer, the world becomes progressively more resistant, more "hard hearted," more violent in response to the message of Jesus. One has the strong sense here of a gathering storm building up in reaction to the gospel and preparing to lash out at the Christ with all the power and might at its disposal. John underscores this image with a vision of the world progressively more hostile and inimical to the kingdom, much like the heart of the Pharaoh was progressively hardened against the pleas of Moses to let the Israelites go free from Egypt. Here sin is not only represented as a power and a force, but as an enemy, as one who is roused by the call of the prophet to a show of diabolical violence. There is, in response to the call to repentance, a conversion to malice.

In our own experience of and reflections upon sin we are cognizant of this dimension. We know that persons do not tend to plateau out indefinitely, but instead either continue to grow and develop or begin to deteriorate. Small decisions set the ground for more serious questions and crises. Virtue and vice have their own logic, their own dynamism, and tend to accelerate, inviting the person to ever deeper levels of commitment or disintegration. We are told from our childhood to avoid venial sins because they can be the occasion for something more serious and truly deadly. The appetite for sin, once awakened, can get insatiable.

In the sense that sin seems to be more than an habitual or regularly occurring problem, in the sense that it seems to be a kind of malignancy which turns more and more toward death, it would seem appropriate to describe sin as pathological. Sin represents a conversion at the core of the person, a conversion that gathers more and more speed as it progresses, a conversion that seems to become more and more irreversible, more set in its ways, a conversion to disintegration and death.

Sin: From Pathology to Virus to Spiral

A Contagious Infection

The notion of sin as a chronic pathology adds two dimensions to our understanding, dimensions which were beyond the parameters of the concept of transgression. However, even this represents an understanding still too confined by the radical individualism of much of our thinking about sin. For we know that human sinfulness does not start or stop in the individual. Instead, the very heart of the tragedy and the horror of human sinfulness is that it is contagious, that the murderously destructive reality of sin passes from one living soul to another. The crime of sin is that we do lead and are led into temptation and indeed into sin; that the sins of the parents are passed onto their children, and to their children's children. For the lived human experience tells us that none of us are "original" sinners, and that we are, as scripture tells us, conceived in sin, born in sin, and raised in an environment rendered noxious and life-threatening by the contagion of sin.

Sin is a virus. For all of our freedom and independence, for all of our precious individuality, we live in a world in which sin is a deadly and contagious virus which threatens, saps, and debilitates our moral and spiritual health and lives. Parents pass sin onto their children, teachers instruct their pupils in it, governments lead their peoples into it. From generation to generation, in all sorts of structures, groupings, games and institutions, sin is passed from one heart to another like a deadly and insidious contagion. Unlike the cancer campaigns, no one is expecting to "wipe out sin in your lifetime."

Kevin O'Shea describes the power and violence of this virus, which he calls "Sin of the world":

> Biblical thought about sin is dominated by the theme of the Sin of the World. We should write it with a capital: the Sin, the Sinfulness of the world. Modern thought about sin is dominated by the idea of the "human act" in which "sin" happens. St. Paul would have called that a "transgression", he would not have called it "Sin". Sin is a deeper thing, a powerful virus of evil which has a history of its own, on the cosmic plane.
>
> The Sin of the world is a virus of evil which entered the world as a personal force through original sin and dynamically unfolds itself and tightens its grip on humanity and on the world in an escalating fashion down the ages of history. It is the hidden power which multiplies transgressions in the history of mankind. They are merely its symptoms; it is greater and deeper than all of them. It forms human history into what we might call "perdition history" (to coin the opposite of "salvation history").[12]

It is not only the pervasive malice of this virus, however, that one notices. The heart of the tragedy here is that in some way the sins of the parents have become the sins of the children, that the children imitate their parents in their idolatry, their injustice, and even their murderous rage against the prophets God has sent to call them back to him. The new and fresh generations are in some way tainted with all of the malice and wickedness of their elders. When this generation dies off evil will not die with it, but will be passed on to the next generation. The viral contagion is a kind of spiral, a cycle of malice that seems bred into the very fiber of human experience, and although it is worsened through the active cooperation of individual persons performing distinct acts of sinfulness, these are but many heads of the same dragon, a dragon who lives beyond generations and individuals. The viral character of sin points to the fact that it is not just personal, it is transpersonal.

Social Sin

In order to fully understand this transpersonal dimension of sin we need momentarily to step beyond the boundaries of individualism or even of the interpersonal and to look at the living organism of the community. For indeed the virus of sin not only threatens the single person or an accumulation of single persons, it threatens the life of the human community. It is a sort of plague which attacks and infects not just isolated individuals, but the very integrity and health of the society. It is in this sense that O'Shea has spoken of sin as a virus. For not only does sin have a personal character which is revealed in its habitual and malignant dimensions, but it also has a social character which we note in its contagiousness.

But how is it then that we can talk meaningfully about sin at this level? How is it possible to continue to believe in the freedom and responsibility of the person, refusing to accept guilt by association or some vague notion of corporate blame or culpability, which often turns out to be some ambiguous class bigotry, and still understand what people are talking about when they refer to "sinful structures"? How can we speak of sin which infects the body politic or covenantal community and which is both real and transpersonal?

In moving from act to habit we recognized that patterns

of behavior normally indicate the presence of a freedom and a decision on a deeper level of the person. Habits were not a denial of the instantaneous freedom of choice experienced in individual decisions, but rather pointed to the way in which this obvious freedom was connected to a more fundamental and personal freedom. So were transgression sins related to vicious sins. In a similar way the individual and conscious freedom of the person stands in a relationship to the freedom of others and indeed in a very real sense the freedom of the community, a relationship that cannot be completely understood or expressed within the confines of personal freedom and sin. The following are some ways of understanding freedom and responsibility on a transpersonal level, opening us up to a consciousness of social sin.

Cooperation, Games and Spirals

Even the most superficial study of human behavior and freedom recognizes the radical situatedness of personal freedom, a condition which influences without eliminating that freedom. Persons live in the world with others. Indeed, much of that world is the community of others among which we live. Personal freedom does not so much operate independently in the world as cooperate in and with the world. While this cooperation is on the one hand an expression of personal freedom, it is also an expression of the radical interdependence of all persons. It is this notion of cooperation which provides an insight into the way in which we can meaningfully talk about sin as transpersonal.

When investigating the ways in which persons cooperate within a group it is useful to employ the notion of a "game." Games describe the habitual patterns of behavior determining the interaction and cooperation among various persons. Games include the rules of conduct and the roles of various agents in play. They also include a basic understanding of the aim or end of the group, and thus of the numerous strategies employed to achieve this or these ends. Game is a level of action beyond either the individual deed or the habitual patterns of a single person. Games represent a grasp of the ways persons behave in and as a group. They describe another level of cooperation.

Certain games, however, tend to be cyclical or repetitive. Such games may be better understood as a sort of spiral in which progressive generations of players are brought into the everlasting game, building upon the effects of past rounds or innings while repeating over and over again the patterns of behavior which have led them this far. Here the cooperation not only tends to be among all the contemporary players, but includes those already gone and not yet arrived.

Family Sin

For example, much of the recent development in the field of "family therapy" is based upon the recognition that to a large degree the "free" responses of persons cannot be fully understood without reference to the family system in which they live and grow, and through which they learn to react to and deal with the world. Studies of the systemic theory of families have made us more aware of the ways in which it is true and useful to speak about such groups not merely as an aggregate whole but as living organisms, each with its own particular methods of dealing with members and outsiders. None of this denies personal freedom, for much of family therapy depends upon the ability of persons to accept insight and move consciously toward change. It does, however, deny a notion of freedom which is radically individualistic and unaware of the cooperative and interdependent character of that freedom.

Particularly do we notice in the study of certain kinds of disturbed families that therapists are refusing more and more to accept the family's definition of one sick or symptomatic family member as the "identified patient." Instead, there is an attempt to examine the ways in which and the levels at which the various persons, groupings and relationships in this family act as enablers, sustaining or empowering diseased behavior. Such cooperation will normally not fall within the range of what we would consider blameworthy. Nonetheless, the cooperation is quite real.[13]

Even more recently there has been a growing interest in the way in which family groupings hand on their patterns of behavior from one generation to the next, and how successive generations are affected by their relation to parents and grandparents, indeed how the children and grandchildren become enablers and co-dependents supporting the ongoing life of disease and disfunction in the family. Much of this recent discussion has been specifically focused around the ways in which each member of the family cooperates in this process in ways that traditional and individualistic therapy had not averted to. Thus, this cooperation can span generations and enable the passing on of unfreedom from elder to child and beyond.

"Groupthink"

Cooperation is also noticeable in the area of corporate activity. Both Karl Menninger and M. Scott Peck offer extended discussions of some of the ways in which corporate bodies or bureaucratic units can be evil, tending to function at a level of morality which we would never tolerate in individual persons. This is true even though each and every member of the group is a conscious and competent adult who knows better than to act in such a fashion. Menninger discusses those characteristics discoverable in a large group which allow it to function in an immoral fashion without any real sense of fault or guilt, characteristics which he notes are part of a certain kind of a "groupthink" or herd mentality.[14] Scott Peck, in his analysis of the phenomenon of "group evil" as exemplified in the Mylai massacre, describes the ways in which individual persons can regress into dependency and narcissism within the setting of certain kinds of groups.[15] Such a phenomenon represents a kind of cooperation in evil or sin on the level of a mob. This does not mean that Peck sees all groups as evil, only that there can be evil or destructive tendencies in certain sorts of groups.[16]

Oppression

Within the past generation there has been a growing discussion among political and liberation theologians about the presence of "structural" sin, referring to the oppressive and unjust economic and political institutions that dominate many of the regimes of different nations and much of the international political/economic order. Such systems are seen as sinful because they have institutionalized oppressive and unjust patterns of behavior, given official sanction and legal status to class, ethnic, racial and religious intolerance, and systematically denied the basic dignity and human rights of persons under the scandalous guise of enforcing law and establishing justice.

It is meaningful to talk about such institutions as evil and sinful in a sense that is more than a mere derivative of personal or actual sinfulness. For such institutions represent the structural establishment and official sanctioning of sinful attitudes and disordered, alienated, and unjust relationships. They are both the full flowering of personal and actual sin as well as the unquenching font from which such sins will ever continue to grow.

The cycle of oppression, moving from injustice to rebellion and onto further repressive violence, is a pattern of sin that volleys between warring parties and spirals from one generation to the next, each learning from and living out the sins of their elders. This is true whether one is speaking about military regimes in Latin America, rock-throwing violence on the streets of Derry and Beirut, or the cancerous growth of nuclear missile silos across the breadbaskets of America and Russia.

Conclusion

The notion of sin as an individual act taken by a person fails to express much of the depth, breadth and dynamism or malignancy of the reality which threatens the life of human persons, both singly and as they live in communities. The crime model offers a snapshot of a human mystery which endures and grows through time, while permeating the fiber of the social structures which constitute the human community. It is necessary to employ models which better express these dimensions of human sinfulness, models that recognize its viral and cyclical character.

Notes

1. This definition and language relies upon the discussion of sin found in Thomas (*Summa Theologiae,* 1a2ae 71,6), who in turn depends on Augustine's definition of sin as "word, deed or desire contrary to the law of God" (*Contra Faustum,* XXII, PL 42, 418).

2. Stanley Hauerwas, *The Peaceable Kingdom* (Notre Dame: University of Notre Dame Press, 1983) 46–49. Timothy O'Connell, "A Theology of Sin," 283–289.

3. John Glaser, "Transition between Sin and Grace: Fresh Perspectives," in *Theological Studies,* vol. 29, 1968, 241–259.

4. Schoonenberg, *Man and Sin,* 111–117.

5. Thomas Aquinas, *Summa Theologiae,* ed. and trans. John Fearon, O.P. (New York: McGraw-Hill, 1969) xvi.

6. Of particular interest here is Louis Monden's work on fundamental option, as well as the role of character in the narrative theology of Stanley Hauerwas.

7. Rather excellent discussions of this question, developing especially its Thomistic roots, are to be found in James Gaffney's *Sin Reconsidered,* 62–64, and Louis Monden's *Sin, Liberty and Law,* 39.

8. See, for example, Henri Rondet's discussion of this in *The Theology of Sin,* 30–32.

9. Franz Böckle *Fundamental Moral Theology* (Dublin: Gill & Macmillan, 1980) 85.

10. William Glasser, *Positive Addiction* (New York: Harper and Row, 1976).

11. Again, Paul's description of the progressive perversion of the pagans in Romans 1:18–32 captures some of the flavor of this idea, as does the growth of sin witnessed in Genesis 3–11.

12. Kevin F. O'Shea, C.SS.R., "The Reality of Sin: A Theological and Pastoral Critique," in *The Mystery of Sin and Forgiveness,* ed. by Michael J. Taylor, S.J. (New York: Alba House, 1971) 94–95.

13. Two texts discussing these notions are: Anne Wilson Schaef, *Co-Dependence: Misunderstood-Mistreated* (Minneapolis: Winston Press, 1986), and Melodie Beattie, *Codependent No More* (New York: Harper and Row, 1987).

14. Karl Menninger, *Whatever Became of Sin?* (New York: Hawthorn Books, 1973) 94–101.

15. M. Scott Peck, *The People of the Lie* (New York: Simon & Schuster, 1983) 223–226.

16. For a discussion of the creative or grace-filled dimension of groups, review Peck's more recent text, *A Different Drum,* on community building and peace-making.

7

■
■

SIN AND SICKNESS

■　　　■　　　■

Some Initial Reflections

We began our discussion with the assertion that sin
■ is a mystery, a fundamental mystery of the experience of evil. But it is not the only such mystery. Disease too
is such a mystery. In sickness and disease persons are confronted with the disturbing and confounding reality of evil.[1]
In fact, in both sin and sickness the human community has
been forced in various ways to grapple with the mystery of
evil that disrupts, burdens and threatens our existence. From
the beginnings of history sin and disease have stymied and
teased the human community, challenging it to come up with
a response to the question of evil.

Nor have these notions developed in isolation of one
another. Instead, it would be truer to say that the concepts
of disease and sin grew up in an often inseparable and usually interdependent relationship. This is true not only in the
earliest periods when both priest and medicine man were
united in the tribal shaman, but continues to be the case in
an age when so much theologizing is being done about the
meaning of illness and health. The study and understanding

of the religious and moral dimension of the human person and community often went hand in hand with a grasp of the health and well-being of the same.[2]

The reasons for this are somewhat simple and straight-forward. In both sin and sickness the mystery of evil threatens to devastate the human person and/or community. Both disease and sin raise some of the same basic issues in the consciousness of the person, demanding that one wrestle with and respond to some basic issues regarding the meaning and nature of life and death. To incarnate human beings the issue of sickness raises serious questions about their relationship to the divine, and even the meaning and identity of that divinity. One can hardly be cognizant of the destructive power of illness without sooner or later postulating certain basic questions about one's relation to the absolute, and the meaning of that absolute. At the same time we have already noted how much of the most primitive reflections upon moral and religious evil are grounded in the experience of physical suffering. The alienating experience of sin is often enough discovered in the pain and disorientation of human suffering and illness.

Even the most cursory investigation of the story of medicine alerts us to several connections between sin and sickness. From the earliest epochs when medicine was dominated by a religio-magical understanding of reality to our current conversations on the contributions of theology to medical ethics it is obvious that the discussions of salvation and healing or of sin and sickness have often been interrelated.

For this reason it might be of some use in the current project of unraveling the meaning of human sinfulness to examine briefly the concept of disease. Perhaps some of the systematic and theological reflections upon this notion will offer a foothold into a better grasp of sin. What are some insights that the notion of disease might offer toward the development of a more adequate understanding of sin? In what ways are the notions related, and how might a "disease" model help us to envision the reality of sin? Most of all, in what way might it be helpful to understand human sinfulness as a disease?

Some Problems

Before moving into a discussion of a "disease" model of sin it is important to take note of a few ways in which the relationship between sin and sickness has been understood in the past and to critique such positions. For some of these understandings would clearly not be helpful in developing a better grasp of sin, or in overcoming certain of the handicaps of the stain, crime or personal models of sin. Briefly, then, we will examine three ways in which disease has been understood in relation to the religious or moral dimension: (a) disease as the wrath/punishment of God, (b) disease as the expression or consequence of personal character, (c) disease as the denial of moral freedom.

Wrath of God: Taboo

In the earliest and most primitive communities disease was often understood as the consequence of a violation of some taboo. The gods in their wrath would lash out at humans for some sacrilege, some violation of the holy or sacred. In such an understanding it was the duty of the medicine man or shaman to discover through omens or oracles the infringement committed and to assign a treatment that would satisfy the displeased deities and return all to a state of health. Sometimes a sacrifice would atone for such sacrileges, while other occasions demanded some form of exile from the holy place or land.

In this grasp of disease as an expression of divine wrath for a violation of sacred laws, there was a strong sense of disease as something that was unholy, unclean, untouchable. And indeed the often disfiguring and untidy characteristic of certain diseases would tend to underscore this "stain" notion, as would the fear and confusion generated by diseases which were contagious. Diseases that were experienced as messy, disfiguring and/or contagious would tend to evoke fears in the local community, fears that would lead to ostracism and lend support to a taboo mentality. Such tendencies continue in our own times in the popular attitudes and responses to Hansen's disease and AIDS.[3]

Wrath of God: Punishment

A later development on the same theme began to see or understand all human suffering and illness as the rather direct result of human sinfulness. In this grasp, reflected in the "friends" of Job and in much of the primitive Puritan attitude in the colonies, all human suffering is deserved by the suffering person or persons. Health and wealth are clear and evident signs of the loving providence of God, while disease is the fruit of sin, whether one's own or that of one's parents. In this attitude the disciples ask Jesus in the gospel of John whether the man born blind was being punished for his sins or the sins of his elders.

Here disease has come to be explained as the consequence of sin, as the result of sinful behavior, as the just reward of an unjust life or action. While not denying a connection between certain forms of behavior and various sorts of illness, this vision needs to be criticized for its oversimplification of the experience of human illness as well as its somewhat arrogant willingness to saddle the sick and suffering with a double burden of illness and guilt—hardly a gospel response. It also tends to assume an innocence on the part of the healthy, confusing soundness of body with sanctity of person. Thus the jogger has become the patron saint of a new phariseeism.

Disease as Character Flaw

In a recent article on "Illness as Metaphor" Susan Sontag discusses the ways a contemporary society has updated the two previous understandings with a psychological interpretation of disease.

> Moreover, there is a peculiarly modern predilection for psychological explanations of disease as of everything else. Psychologizing seems to provide control over the experience and events (like grave illnesses) over which people have in fact little or no control. Psychological understanding undermines the "reality" of a disease.[4]

What Sontag finds particularly disturbing in this tendency is that the process of psychologizing a disease tends to discover the root meaning or cause of the illness in the mind or character of the patient. Thus, the cancer patient is responsible for his disease because he has not appropriately expressed his suppressed emotions, as the TB patient had been culpable of not having sufficient passions. The stress upon such psychological interpretations renders the patient responsible for his illness and assumes that those with sufficient will, appropriate emotive responses or vital personalities will survive infection, contamination or contagion. Once again we are dealing with a vision that assumes that the ill person is responsible for his sickness, and that such sickness is a consequence of his character, a sort of psychological wrath of the gods.

Disease as "Unfreedom"

Gerald McHugh, in a text on *Christian Faith and Criminal Justice,* addresses the folly of what he refers to as the "treatment" theory of penology. According to McHugh, the psychological approach of much penal theory is heavily deterministic and behavioristic, paying no attention to the freedom of the prisoners. Indeed, McHugh argues, such "treatment" theories currently in practice deny or ignore personal freedom and moral responsibility of any sort, and aim at modifying behavior in ways that patently violate the dignity and freedom of the prisoners. The justification offered by such theorists is that the prisoners are "ill." In such an understanding sickness is perceived as identical with complete lack of responsibility. The sick person is totally powerless, lacking any freedom. As such he need not be engaged or treated as a person, but is to be moved about the board like a chess pawn.

Such a view of illness, incredibly simplistic, fails to take seriously the freedom and dignity of the sick person, and assumes that sickness is the exact opposite of responsibility, that the sick person is per se not responsible. Hence, the sick are not only innocent, they are absent, passive, vacant tools to be utilized by responsible agents. For the ill there are not moral issues, having neither freedom nor responsibility. The sick are not moral or immoral. They are amoral.

A Critique of These Views

The problem with the wrath of God theories is primarily that they are grounded in fear and ignorance. This is true whether the interpretation is one of taboo, guilt or psychology. As medicine developed an accurate understanding of the physiological etiology of different diseases the community experienced such illnesses less and less as mysterious or divinely inspired. As the cures for such diseases were discovered, the fears generated by their contagion evaporated. Persons came to know the real (single) cause of such illnesses and the effective treatment. This lowered the fears and made quarantine and divinization obsolete. In short, diseases were believed to be caused by God to the degree that their physical cause was not understood and/or a cure was not available.

Even today diseases like cancer (and AIDS) provoke either theological or psychological interpretations to the degree that persons experience them as of unknown (or multiple) origin or having no known cure.

At the same time the behaviorist response of "treatment" therapy is guilty of oversimplification in the other direction. To impose an exclusively deterministic "disease" model is in flagrant denial of the fact of human freedom, and leads one to behave in a way that denies, ignores and violates personal freedom and dignity. Such a vision is unacceptable.

Sin as a Disease

Given some of the limits and problems of certain ways in which the relationship between sin and sickness has been understood in the past, one is faced with the question as to whether or not the notion of disease has anything to offer to the present discussion on models of sin. Can the notion of disease offer any insights into a better or richer understanding of the mystery of human sinfulness?

If we are able to discard the concept of sickness as the wrath of God or the expression of a character flaw, as well as transcend a narrowly deterministic grasp of disease as employed in certain treatment theories, it may be possible to discover some contributions that a "disease" model of sin could make to the current crisis. To that end let us examine the notion of sin as "disease."

Some Biblical Roots

The stance Jesus takes against juridical thinking and postures of self-righteous innocence does not ignore sin. There is no attempt to dismiss the reality or pervasiveness of the malice of sin. Instead, his life and ministry is a constant struggle with the crippling and disintegrating power of sin, a power from which he has come to save a humanity (personal and communal) which cannot save itself. In fact, far from dismissing the reality of sin, the scandal which Jesus' reconciling ministry constitutes for the righteous "innocent" is to be found specifically in his employment of a profound and religious sense of sin. For instead of accepting a juridical notion of sin which dichotomizes communities into the guilty and the innocent, Jesus argues that the reality of sin is the universal experience of being alienated from and in need of the loving mercy of God. Thus he shatters the pseudo-innocence of those around him and calls them to be about the process of conversion.

Within the gospels Jesus often employs the model of sin as disease and sinner as one who is suffering from an illness. Referring to himself as a physician and his ministry as one of healing (Lk 5:31), Christ continues to reinforce this model through the tight association between healing and forgiveness in his preaching and miracles (Lk 5:18–26). This notion of sin as illness instead of crime seems to be a major way in which Jesus contrasts his grasp of sin and forgiveness with that of his contemporaries, which would indicate that such a model could act as an effective corrective to the limits and violence of juridical thinking.[5]

Biblical theology offers support to this disease model in that the latter is coherent with a wider scope of biblical thought on sin. While western individualism has tended to focus upon the concept of transgression found in scripture (Gal 3:19; Rom 5:14; Mk 11:25), such individualism has been less interested in or adept at employing the notions of sin as power or sin as state, major biblical analogies of the mystery of sin.[6]

Sin as a state, a chronic reality persisting through the story of the person, and sin as power, a disintegrating experience threatening the core freedom of the person, represent fundamental biblical insights into the experience of human sinfulness. To such dimensions of sin the analogy of disease seems better suited than that of crime. The disease model speaks much more accurately about the radical ways in which sin can contextualize the experience of freedom and responsibility, illustrating better the situated and limited liberty of the person. The admixture of freedom and determinism which constitutes lived human experience is better explained in categories of illness.

The disease model also avoids the extrinsicism of juridical categories. Sin as illness is coherent with the notions of sin as state and power in that both sorts of models point to the fact that sin pervades the human experience. Sin is not merely something one does, an act performed or a crime committed. It is also, even primarily, an orientation toward disintegration and death. Sin permeates the totality of the human experience, contaminating all with its noxious presence and influence, destabilizing human efforts at growth, development and integration and tempting the disoriented persons and communities to further and further disintegration.

Some Advantages

Not only does this disease model find ample support in the gospel narratives of Jesus' ministry and the broader reflections of biblical theology, but it offers several advantages in the development of a theology of human sinfulness: (1) it is oriented to healing/forgiveness instead of judgment/ punishment; (2) its grasp of forgiveness is more realistic; (3) the language of illness better illustrates the religious experience of sin; (4) a sound etiology of the illness of sin replaces the violence of individualistic and juridical categories.

Forgiveness

Criminals are to be punished, normally with severity, often with brutalizing violence. On the other hand the sick are to be the recipients of the most tender human mercy and care. The disease model is employed by Jesus at least in part because such a model orients one to a response of healing care and loving forgiveness. Whatever the appropriate response to sin, it is clear that the Christian response to the sinner is reconciliation and forgiveness. By underscoring the powerlessness, disorientation and weakness of the sinner this model invites compassion and mercy for one who is lost, as opposed to judgment and punishment for one who is evil.[7]

In this way it seems clear that the disease model is more coherent with the liberating, reconciling and loving God of the scriptures, more in touch with a rich and vibrant theology of the graciousness of God and more effective in offering a Christian response to the mystery of sin and the experience of the sinner.

This insight is of particular import for a full understanding of moral theology itself. Insofar as a disease model orients theology and the church away from judgment and toward healing will the field of theological ethics be understood as truly pastoral and not simply clinical or analytical. For far from passing judgment from a detached and objective point of view, the moralist is committed to the healing of the persons and communities suffering from sin. Only in this way can moral theology avoid the judgment of levying burdens without lifting fingers. To the degree that the disease model keeps moral theology from being a science of the pathology of sin and moves it in the direction of healing the persons and communities who suffer from the illness of sin is it superior to previous juridical categories.

Realism

The disease model also provides a more realistic notion of forgiveness than the criminal model. For in the notion of sin as crime forgiveness becomes a juridical act by which the penitent is pardoned for his misdeeds. His guilt is expunged and in some fashion he is returned to a state of original innocence. According to this model, through either the act of forgiveness or the payment of a debt, the scales of justice are returned to their original state of balance.

In either case the juridical categories tend to present forgiveness as a fairly extrinsic experience, having little to do with a real conversion of the sinner and implying a somewhat magical grasp of forgiveness as the wiping clean of the slate and the return to an original state of innocence. Instead of eliminating sin by projecting it out onto the individual criminals, juridical models in this case claim to expunge sin not only from the person's soul but also from the human story.

But history is not rewritten or unwritten by forgiveness. Nor is sin (and all its effects) erased. Only in a highly magical and extrinsic understanding of sin and forgiveness could such a stance be maintained. Juridical understandings of sin tend to operate in a taboo sort of framework where the stain of sin can be avoided through projection, or washed away through forgiveness.[8]

Healing offers a more realistic grasp of the process of forgiveness, a process in which one does not struggle so much for a recapturing of lost innocence as for an integration and animation of an alienated and pathological organism. In the healing of disease there is a new synthesis of the disparate and sick parts of the organism, achieving a new homeostasis.

According to this model of sin, therefore, forgiveness is an integrative and reconciling process in which the sinner moves toward a new "whole-ness" which includes and transcends the experience of sin. Confession becomes the self-acceptance of the totality of one's story, the embracing of all parts, virtuous and sinful, in an act of faith in the forgiving love of God, an act that believes there can be a new generation of life. Thus, in the very soil where sin abounds, grace abounds all the more.

Genuine forgiveness is not about a simple pardoning or forgetting of sins, but about empowering the sinner to an experience of conversion through which there can be an integration of the whole of human experience.[9]

Weakened Freedom

A third advantage of the disease model is the fact that it highlights the awareness of moral theology concerning the weakness and neediness of the sinner before the power and malice of sin. A profoundly religious sense of sin, unlike a simply moral one, situates the sinner in a relational context where sin points to his radical weakness and to the need for the redemptive and forgiving activity of a loving God. To perceive sin as an illness and not merely as the act of a free will is to understand that one will need help in overcoming this chronic, debilitating and pathological experience. To confess sin as an illness before the God who was rejected is to make an act of faith in the mercy and liberating grace of that God. Thus, the model of sin as a disease, by underscoring the pervasive need which the sinner has for an integrating and healing reconciliation, is more likely to avoid the moralistic notions of a juridical vision and to embrace a stance of hope-filled faith confessing a profound dependence upon the healing God of mercy.[10]

Contagion

Finally, contagion and etiology are essential elements of the notion of disease, elements which, when applied to the

concept of human sinfulness, provide a more dynamic, syn-
thetic and realistic grasp of the origins, manifestations and
consequences of this mystery. Regardless of the individualistic presumption of the juridical model, sin does not blossom
full-blown and original within the limited confines of the
individual free will. Instead, sin precedes the response of the
free will, contextualizes its experience of liberty and reaches
beyond its intended expression in all sorts of consequences
and sinfulness. Persons can choose with limited and often
impaired freedom to cooperate or not with this mystery, to
contribute or not to its power. Nonetheless, each person and
generation is born into a story and context made noxious by
sin's presence. There is no need to reinvent the apple.

The disease model of sin underscores the importance of
the ongoing context of sin in which all persons find themselves and by which they experience themselves as disoriented, weakened and impaired.

Contemporary Roots of a "Disease" Model

Within the social sciences the shift from criminal to disease categories can be seen in attempts to understand numerous forms of conduct as symptomatic of some psychological,
physiological or social illness. Developments in biology as
well as depth and social psychology illustrating the numerous
ways in which human freedom is profoundly impaired have
led many within the social sciences to understand more how
the human person's destructive behavior may well be an expression of a disorder for which he is not culpable in any criminal sense. To this deepened grasp of man's situated freedom
language about disease seems more appropriate and useful.

Although certain moves in this area have been understood (or misunderstood) as attempts to abandon any sense of personal responsibility, thus rendering "criminals" innocent by reason of insanity, it would be simplistic to dismiss these developments so lightly. Significant evidence exists illustrating the role and import of biological, psychological and social determinants that profoundly impair the felt experience of freedom described by those whom society classifies as criminals.[11] Even authors critical of treatment or therapy models of penology subscribing to a Skinnerian denial of personal freedom or responsibility have argued that human sinfulness is a moral illness more than a freely committed crime.[12]

One of the most interesting experiences related to the disease model of sin has been the development and high success rate of the Alcoholics Anonymous program and the contention of this therapy that alcoholism is a disease. There are a number of elements that make this statement particularly relevant to the present discussion, not the least of which is the phenomenal success AA has had in helping alcoholics to recover. Reports indicate that AA has had a higher recovery ratio than any other program or approach, a fact further attested to by the incorporation of the AA techniques and philosophy into numerous other therapeutic programs founded since and treating a number of personal disorders. The twelve steps of the program have even been incorporated into texts on spiritual formation and growth. The disease model, a constitutive element of the AA approach, is clearly an effective therapeutic tool in bringing the alcoholic to recovery. This alone might be reason to embrace such a model.[13]

Authors in this field suggest that the disease model aids in the recovery of the alcoholic by intervening to break up the disintegrating cycle of alcoholic behavior, i.e., abusive drinking—guilt/remorse—alienating self-hatred—renewed self-destructive drinking. The high degree of moralism found in many alcoholics acts as a contributing cause to the progressively disintegrating power of the disease. By illustrating the degree to which the drinker's freedom is impaired by the chronic, debilitating and pathological illness from which he suffers, AA attempts to shift him out of a moralistic stance, a stance which has not only not proven helpful in freeing the person but has actually contributed to the problem.[14]

Thus, the disease model is not employed to encourage the alcoholic to abandon moral responsibility or to dismiss the ethical dimension of alcoholism. Instead, this model helps drinkers to recognize the limits of their freedom and the character of their responsibility, to understand the power which this destructive disease has in and over their lives and the lives of their families, and to perceive the need to quit "playing God" and hand themselves over in faith to their "higher power."[15] This means that AA has deliberately and effectively employed the disease model to empower millions of persons (and through Al Anon millions of families) to be liberated from a chronic and deadly disease of the body, mind and soul. Clearly the strengths of this model, as employed by AA, are in its realistic grasp of contextualized human freedom and responsibility, its orientation toward healing and reconciliation, and its abiding faith and trust in the mercy, grace and power of God. It would be hard to imagine a more adequate and practical grasp of the experience of sin, grace and forgiveness than that of AA.

Criticism: Irresponsibility

The most serious criticism of the disease model is that it leads to an abandonment of a sense of sin by relieving persons of any responsibility for their actions. By reducing sin to categories of illness this model supposedly accepts an exclusively determinist position, denying the existence of personal freedom and rendering the ethical dimension irrelevant. Such an argument, although representing serious over-simplifications, is too significant to ignore and needs to be responded to in some depth.

In small part the criticism is well founded. Certain psychologists, sociologists and penologists either deny human freedom outright or espouse anthropologies which so severely undercut the notions of personal freedom and responsibility as to render them meaningless. Some utilize disease models to explain every form of destructive behavior in a fashion absolving persons of any responsibility, only at the cost of reducing these persons to automatons. "Liberated" penologists of this century have employed radical behaviorist "therapies" which treated the criminal-patient by systematically by-passing or attempting to destroy his personal freedom.[16] The behaviorist control and psycho-surgery of Stanley Kubrick's "A Clockwork Orange" and Ken Kesey's "One Flew Over the Cuckoo's Nest" reveal the stark immorality and inhumanity of such approaches. One can sense the rage of those treated as merely passive carriers of disease and is reminded, as Paul Ramsey has noted, that patients are persons.

However, such relatively extreme positions are quite rare among the social sciences, and much of the above argument of irresponsibility is based upon inaccurate caricatures of the insights of depth and social psychology. Psychology does not normally tend toward an abandonment of personal freedom and responsibility, only toward a contextualization of these notions in response to the moralism and guilt-complexes it perceives within traditional religious teaching on sin and as a result of various insights into the limited character of that freedom and (thus) responsibility.[17]

One of the reasons for both this disproportionate reaction to a shift toward a disease model of sin and the simplistic characterization of contemporary psychology's critique of the guilt-complex as an abandonment of accountability is that juridical models of sin allow for such a narrow grasp of personal freedom and responsibility. According to the criminal model responsibility is reduced to individual culpability for the commission of a sin-crime. And although individual culpability is *one* sort of responsibility, it clearly does not exhaust the meaning of this notion. The fact that the jurist is concerned exclusively with establishing the criminal guilt or innocence of the defendant and cannot sentence or punish a person whose degree of accountability does not constitute penal culpability does not mean that there can be no other discussion of personal responsibility. Depth and social psychology, along with the disease model of sin, are open to and employ a wide range of understandings of the ways in which and degrees to which persons can be both free and responsible.[18]

Indeed, the juridical categories tend to artificially dichotomize reality into the guilty and the innocent by a strict reliance on these very limited and unrealistic notions of responsibility and freedom. The disease model, especially with aid of insights provided from psychology, is able to transcend this dichotomizing trend and speak of a wide range of experiences of freedom and responsibility. Far from dismissing these notions, the disease model is capable of articulating a broader variety of ways in which they might be understood and experienced.

Nor is this true only of a psychological grasp of illness and responsibility. General medicine also knows of a number of relationships between diseases and responsibility.

Without regressing to a simplistic understanding of disease as divine retribution for human sinfulness (either the person's or his ancestor's), contemporary medicine is aware that much of the experience of human illness in the twentieth century is the rather direct fruit of human decisions made on the personal and societal levels.[19] Preventive medicine and environmental studies indicate again and again the correlation between decisions about global ecology, individual lifestyles and personal habits, to name a select few, and the resulting increase in all sorts of diseases and illnesses, from malnutrition and starvation to heart disease and lung cancer. Again, the correlation is not usually immediate, overwhelmingly clear, or one-to-one, so the grasp of responsibility is more nuanced, varied, and complicated. But this does not mean that there is no responsibility, only that the understanding of this responsibility must exceed the grasp of individual criminal culpability.

Even within the highly individualistic framework of the doctor-patient dyad medicine depends for its success upon a number of "responsible" actions or responses by the patient. The simple identification of a person with an illness does not situate him or her in a completely passive or irresponsible context. The persons who are patients share in the cooperative efforts of medicine, from prevention to recovery. The ill person is called to exercise responsibility in a number of ways, each of them facilitating the healing process. Individuals who fail to take preventive measures, who develop unhealthy patterns of diet, work or exercise, who ignore or deny warning symptoms from their bodies, who hide symptoms from their physicians, who refuse or fail to cooperate in treatment plans, or who quickly abandon regimens prescribed as part of a recovery program are behaving irresponsibly. The very fact that moral medicine is not simply a professional ethics for physicians and other health care personnel reveals that there are significant moral questions and responsibilities for the patient as well.[20] There is no reason to believe that a disease model of sin relieves the person of all responsibility. A diabetic is not culpable for his disease, but he clearly experiences responsibility in dealing with its presence and maintaining a balanced and healthy life in the face of it.

Again, the employment of the disease model by AA might prove relevant to a response to this criticism. For here too some have argued that the description of alcoholism as a disease eliminates the ethical issue and encourages further irresponsibility from the drinker. The fact is, however, that the disease model produces just the opposite effect. For while the notion of alcoholism as a disease is intentionally employed to relieve the alcoholic of a disproportionate, unrealistic and crippling sense of guilt, such a contextualization of personal freedom serves the function of empowering the weakened person to take more responsibility for his actual freedom.[21]

Far from calling the alcoholic to abandon responsibility, the success of the AA program rests upon the free and cooperative efforts of addicted drinkers struggling in a supportive and nurturing context to overcome their addiction, progressively developing and actualizing their shattered freedom and responsibility. The disease model, by offering a more realistic grasp of the drinker's diminished freedom and responsibility, actually enables the addicted person to behave with more responsibility and freedom. The recovery rate of AA and its imitators illustrates the effectiveness of this model.[22]

In conclusion, the shift from a juridical understanding of sin as a crime to a medical one of sin as an illness offers a number of significant advantages: (1) a more realistic and contextualized grasp of the breadth of personal freedom and responsibility; (2) a profound and effective orientation away from an alienating and punitive violence, which contributes to sin's disintegrating power, toward a process of healing, forgiveness and reconciliation; (3) a fuller grasp of the theology of sin revealed in scripture and integrated with dogmatic theology's insights on grace. Concerns that this shift has contributed to a loss of a sense of sin through the abandonment of personal freedom and responsibility seem largely uninformed and unwarranted.

Notes

1. Schoonenberg, *Man and Sin*, 40–47.
2. One excellent study on this relationship is found in Martin E. Marty and Kenneth L. Vaux (eds.), *Health/ Medicine and the Faith Traditions* (Philadelphia: Fortress Press, 1982).
3. Douglas Shenson, "When Fear Conquers," in *The New York Times Magazine*, February 28, 1988, 34–38, 48.
4. Susan Sontag, "Illness as Metaphor," *The New York Review*, February 9, 1978, 29.
5. Rondet, *The Theology of Sin*, 22–29.
6. Eugene La Verdiere, S.S.S., "The Need for Salvation: A New Testament Perspective." *Chicago Studies* 21:3 (1982) 233f; Alphonse Spilly, C.P.P.S., "Sin and Alienation in the Old Testament: The Personalist Approach," *Chicago Studies*, 21:3 (1982) 215; Schoonenberg, *Man and Sin*, 101; Rondet, *The Theology of Sin*, 29–38; Kevin O'Shea, C.S.S.R., "The Reality of Sin: A Theological and Pastoral Critique," *The Mystery of Sin and Forgiveness*, 92–98; Böckle, *Fundamental Moral Theology*, 100.

7. O'Connell, "A Theology of Sin," 291.

8. Kevin Condon, "The Sense of Sin," *Irish Theological Quarterly* 49:3 (1982) 162–166; Kerans, *Sinful Social Structures*, 47f; May, *Power and Innocence*, 47–64, 210; Monden, *Sin, Liberty and Law*, 154–156; Rigali, "Sin in a Relational World," 331.

9. Raymond Stovich, "Psychology and Salvation: Reflections upon the Human Condition," *Chicago Studies*, 21:3 (1982) 262; O'Connell, "A Theology of Sin," 291; George J. Dyer, "The Need for Salvation: A Pastoral Perspective," *Chicago Studies* 21:3 (1982) 293–306; John Coventry, "Sixteenth and Twentieth Century Concepts of Sin," *The Way Supplement*, 48 (1983) 55; John A. Sanford, *Evil: The Shadow Side of Reality* (New York: Crossroad, 1981) 67–84.

10. Monden, *Sin, Liberty and Law*, 160; Condon, *The Sense of Sin*, 162.

11. McHugh, *Christian Faith and Criminal Justice*, 166–170.

12. Menninger, *Whatever Became of Sin?* 74–93.

13. Howard J. Clinebell, Jr., *Understanding and Counseling the Alcoholic* (Nashville: Abingdon, 1978) 119.

14. Vernon E. Johnson, *I'll Quit Tomorrow* (New York: Harper & Row, 1973) 2; Clinebell, *Understanding and Counseling the Alcoholic*, 178.

15. Clinebell, *Understanding and Counseling the Alcoholic*, 129.

16. McHugh, *Christian Faith and Criminal Justice*, 120–124; Menninger, *Whatever Became of Sin?* 74–93.

17. Schiffers, "Guilt and Moral Evil in Light of the Study of Behavior," 56–58; Henri Niel, "The Limits of Responsibility," in *Sin*, Bernard Murchland (trans.) (New York: Macmillan, 1962) 53f.

18. Bruce Narramore, "The Concept of Responsibility

in Psychopathology and Psychotherapy," *Journal of Psychology and Theology* 13 (1985) 92–94; O'Connell, "Sense of Sin in the Modern World," 19–20.

19. Gene Outka, "Social Justice and Equal Access to Health Care," in *Love and Society: Essays in the Ethics of Paul Ramsey* (Missoula: Scholars Press, 1974) 192; Thomas Wall, *Medical Ethics: Basic Moral Issues* (Washington, D.C.: University Press of America, 1980) 153, 162; James Childress, *Priorities in Biomedical Ethics.* (Philadelphia: Westminster Press, 1981) 79f.

20. Paul Ramsey, *Patient as Person: Explorations in Medical Ethics* (New Haven: Yale University Press, 1970) 116, 118, 130; Bernard Häring, *Medical Ethics* (Slough, England: St. Paul Publications, 1971) 199.

21. Clinebell, *Understanding and Counseling the Alcoholic,* 132–143.

22. *Ibid.,* 167–178.

8
.
:

Sin as an Addiction
■   ■   ■

Introduction: Why Addiction?

Supposing that sin is a sort of illness, a kind of moral
■ sickness. What kind? If one of the goals of a disease
model is to move from a punitive to a therapeutic response,
there is a need for some diagnosis, some understanding of
the type, structure and pathology of the sickness called sin.
Treatment and cure will depend on an accurate understanding of the malaise in question. What sort of sickness is sin?
Let me suggest that sin is an addiction.

Why an addiction? In the course of this chapter several
reasons will be offered for this choice, but three points might
be mentioned here. To begin with, addictions include a
moral dimension. Research continues to show that addiction
is a disease of the whole person, simultaneously operating on
the physical, emotional, and mental as well as spiritual
planes. Thus, perhaps more so than other diseases, addiction
is concerned with both human freedom and the moral dimension. At the same time, however, studies on addiction repeat-
edly reveal just how situated, limited and contextualized this

very freedom actually is.[1] Secondly, the burgeoning data on co-dependence, co-addiction, addictive families and addictive societies provides verifiable evidence concerning the ways in which addiction operates on the personal, familial and societal levels as well as the manner in which addiction is communicated from generation to generation.[2] The use of such a model might go a long way toward explaining how sin operates on these various levels (including social and structural sin), as well as offering a theory of the communication of sin which does not rely upon an association with sexuality. Both of these would be a real benefit. Finally, it is going to be suggested that there is a striking structural similarity between idolatry and addiction, and that human sinfulness in its depth and breadth operates in a mode which has become all too familiar to those working with addicts and addictions of every sort.[3]

Before going any further, however, two major points need to be made, one concerning the approach of this chapter and one addressing the methodology employed in addiction research.

The argument of this chapter is that human sinfulness is a kind of addiction. Insights and information gained by those suffering from, as well as living and working with, addiction are being employed to explain the nature of human sinfulness. All too often in the past churches and clerics, ignorant (sometimes invincibly) of the facts about and detached from the experience of addiction, have spoken about the guilt of the addict. These moralistic homilies have tended to presume an unrealistic amount of freedom and to induce further and unneeded guilt, which all too often enabled the addicts to continue in their downward spiral.

The goal of this chapter is to listen to the voices of those who have recently "learned" so much about addiction, and to use this information in helping us to come to grips with the most destructive human malaise, sin.

Methodologically, the work done on addiction has been very different from the classical approach of Catholic moral theology to the study of sin, an approach which has been characterized as clerical, theoretical, and juridical. Instead, much of the work on addiction has been done by communities of amateurs. The foundational and revolutionary research and development in addiction has often been done by groups of persons not professionally trained in psychology, medicine, theology or philosophy. One author has noted that such professionals have tended until very recently to be a major hindrance to this work. Secondly, these amateurs have "known" about addiction first-hand. They have lived with and recognized their addictions and are driven by a commitment to effective therapeutic action, not to analysis or judgment. And, finally, their work has been singularly effective. AA and other groups like it have produced and honed a program which has been effective in the treatment and cure of millions of addicts of all differing sorts and types.[4]

It would seem, therefore, that addicts and the "study" of addiction may have some real insights (concerning content and method) to offer to a community committed to better understand and pastorally help all of those suffering from the addiction of sin.

This chapter will present the addiction model of sin in three steps. The initial stage will be to investigate the notion of addiction, reviewing some attempts at definition and examining some of the basic elements of this phenomenon. In the second part we will look at the ways in which sin operates as an addiction, focusing upon four specific examples. The final brief section will list some of the advantages of this model.

Addiction: A Developing Paradigm for Sin

But what is addiction? To argue persuasively that sin would be better understood using an addiction model, instead of a stain or crime one, it will be necessary to get a fairly adequate grasp of the notion. To this end let us investigate some of the current material on addiction, looking at some definitions, as well as inquiring into the cycles, characteristics, types, and levels of addiction.

Some Definitions

In the discussion of the disease concept of alcoholism addiction has been described as a "spiritual, psychological, emotional and physical disease. This disease is chronic and progressive and is often noted by a relapse. If it is not interrupted, the disease will cause death or insanity."

Patrick Carnes, in his work on sexual addictions, has described addiction as "a pathological relationship with a mood altering substance," though this would also be true of addictive processes and relationships. Carnes points out that within this pathological relationship the addict believes that he/she has found a constant, repeatable and ultimately dependable substance which is capable of relieving the pain of life by introducing a "happiness" solution.[5]

David Smith (Haight Ashbury Clinic) describes an addiction as the compulsive use of a substance or involvement in a process in spite of its painful and unreasonable consequences.

Others have pointed out that within an addiction the person continues to rely on the substance or process to resolve problems long after it has become counter-productive and inordinately destructive.[6]

Howard Clinebell describes an addict as anyone whose addiction interferes frequently or continuously with any of his important life adjustments and interpersonal relationships.[7]

Anne Wilson Schaef defines an addiction as

> any process over which we are powerless. It takes control of us, causing us to do and think things that are inconsistent with our personal values and leading us to become progressively more compulsive and obsessive. A sure sign of an addiction is the sudden need to deceive ourselves and others—to lie, deny and cover up. An addiction is anything we feel tempted to lie about. An addiction is anything we are not willing to give up (we may not have to give it up and we must be willing to do so to be free of the addiction).[8]

From these various insights a rough draft of the phenomenon of addiction might be sketched out. Addiction would seem to be a pathological relationship with a (normally) mood altering substance or process. Over the short term this substance or process promises the "user" a consistent, dependable and repeatable solution to the anxieties and pains of life, a "fix" if you will. A belief system builds up around the user's relationship to his/her addiction and its increasing importance. As the person becomes more and more immersed in and dependent upon this substance or process he/she experiences himself/herself as less free, more compulsive.

At the same time the addictive process begins to produce
tangible and painful side-effects or consequences. More of
the substance or process is required to kill the pain, a good
deal of which is now being introduced by the very use of the
addictive substance or process. A cycle is in place. The solution has become the problem, but continues to be employed
as if it were a solution.

In order to continue to use the addictive solution and
maintain the addictive belief system the person must now
engage in all sorts of denial and deception to ignore its
counter-productivity and painfulness. Alcohol addicts refer
to this as "stinking thinking," while Carnes names it "impaired thinking." It is the logic necessary to maintain the
house of cards that addictive life has become.

Driven by the growing compulsion the addict feels com-
pelled to lie about behavior, act out in ways which violate
his/her belief system and find other causes (projection) for
the crescendoing pain. This behavior leads inevitably to the
disintegration of all major personal and social relationships,
interferes with and then destroys the user's ability to function in the workplace, and effectively alienates him/her from
all other persons. The addiction operates as a chronic and
progressive disease, disintegrating the physical, spiritual,
emotional and psychological life of the person, leading inevitably to insanity and/or death.

The Cycle of Addiction

Like an AA meeting, most of the works on addiction
include lots of stories. At first fascinating and terrible to
novice ears, these gothic tales of woe soon take on a certain
almost predictable structure. After a while patterns of the

various paths to hell emerge and one has a sense of a long slow spiral into death.

Although, to paraphrase Tolstoy, each unhappy addict is unhappy in his own way, most authors point to a nearly universal cyclical pattern which tends to emerge ad nauseam, or, better yet, unto death. Indeed, the addictive cycle might be defined as a "conversion unto death," a pathological, progressive and chronic disintegration of the whole person.

Carnes, in describing the addictive system of the sexual addict, attempts to show the cyclical path through which such persons progressively disintegrate.[9] He employs a double cycle model, wherein the person's addictive belief system feeds into and is fed by the addictive behavior system.

The addict begins with a set of beliefs, which Carnes describes as including the following four assumptions:

1. I am worthless, bad, evil.
2. No one can love me as I am.
3. No one can dependably meet my needs.
4. The addictive substance or process is my most important need.

Based on these assumptions persons understand and interpret reality, as well as make decisions about how to behave in the world.

The above assumptions lead to impaired thinking, including all sorts of projections, delusions, defense systems and denial mechanisms. Such thinking, based upon the above set of negative beliefs, triggers the addictive behavioral cycle.

Addictive behavior begins with a preoccupation with the addictive substance or process. Carnes describes this fixation as "a trance or mood wherein the addicts minds are completely engrossed with the thoughts of sex," though it could be any substance or process. In this state the addict becomes obsessed with the thought of satisfaction.

Preoccupation leads to a ritualizing process in which the addict moves through a set of patterned practices aimed at intensifying the intoxicating effects of this obsessive state. From this vertigo-inducing precipice the addict moves swiftly into action, using the addictive substance or process, getting high. Shortly therafter comes the crash, oppressing the person with a crippling sense of despair and shame over both his/her addiction and the powerlessness to overcome it.

From such despair persons feel themselves driven to further addictive behavior, looking for some "hair of the dog that bit them." This can be for all sorts of reasons—perhaps to escape the present pain, possibly because it really doesn't matter what one does, or often enough to further punish the worthless and hateful self. A cycle is in place.

The cumulative effect of this addictive behavioral cycle renders one's life progressively more unmanageable. This unmanageability tends to reinforce the negative assumptions of one's belief system, leading to further impaired thinking, more addictive behavior and increased unmanageability. Thus, the addictive belief system leads to the addictive behavioral system, which in turn leads back to the addictive belief system. The rapidly accelerating cycle becomes a closed system feeding upon itself and devouring the addict.

Other authors employ different models to describe addiction, but a reliance upon cyclical or spiral images is fairly consistent.[10] It is not possible to establish that all persons enter the spiral at the same point or to show that one step kicks off the process. However, by the time an addiction is in full bloom, the deadly merry-go-round seems to include all or most of the elements discussed above.

On the personal level this cyclical character of addiction

points to its progressive nature. Addictions begin by seeming to offer a solution to a person's pain. Later they become a part of that pain, and finally they become the most significant and deadly problem confronting the person. Unfortunately, the nature of the addictive belief system renders the addict blind to this reality and persuades him/her to continue to resolve all problems by relying on the addiction solution. This error leads inevitably to insanity and/or death.

On the interpersonal or societal level (to be discussed below) the cycle of addiction highlights the ways in which such compulsions are handed on to successive generations, political parties and governments. Such a model helps one to understand how the abuse of alcohol, sexual activity or other persons can be passed from parent to child. It also offers insights into the ways that revolutionary political parties and governments so often tend to imitate their retired, exiled or assassinated predecessors, something Dickens told us in *The Tale of Two Cities*.[11]

The Addictive Character

There is a great deal of well-founded resistance to attempts to formulate an addictive personality type, as such attempts may well miss the point that anyone can become an addict (or co-dependent) of one sort or another, or indeed of many sorts. Nonetheless, as the addictive cycle unfolds a number of characteristics of addiction tend to surface in a regular, repeatable fashion. For this reason it is possible to speak about the addictive character, while always recognizing that the configuration of these "traits" will be distinct in every user (individual, family or society).[12]

The first thing to note about the addictive character is

that it is insane and deadly, characterized in large part by massive confusion, profound dualism and a progressive pathology. This underscores the disintegrative function of addiction, a function which tears the person apart at every level. The behavior and thought patterns of the addict are blatantly inconsistent and flagrantly out of touch with real life. Addiction does not so much create a new personality as it predictably destroys whatever integration is currently present.

The addictive character tends to evidence a number of the following traits in its progress toward disintegration:[13]

(a) Deception. Denial, projection and delusion constitute the unholy trinity of addiction. In order to justify irrational thought and behavior it is necessary to block out painful information, create and maintain an unreal world, and affix blame for all bad news on any source except the self or the addiction. At all costs there can be no admission of a problem with the self or the addictive substance or process.

(b) Ethical Deterioration. The addictive cycle inevitably leads to moral bankruptcy. The addict violates his/her basic values in thought, word and deed, leading to an intolerable schism of the soul. The lies, self-centeredness and increasing injustice so necessary to sustain the pathology of addiction cause an ongoing deterioration of the ethical spirit of the addict. A cycle of failure, remorse, failure dominates this moral pathology.

(c) Dependence. Aside from the developing pathological dependence on their addiction, dependence also characterizes the network of oppressive, manipulative, alienating and enmeshed relationships in which addicts and their codependents find themselves. Open, honest relationships evidencing a high degree of mutuality, equality and healthy interdependence are impossible for the addict.

(d) Self-Centered. With the progression of the addictive

cycle persons become exclusively obsessed with the self, caring little for others. Indeed, other persons are considered only to the degree that they can aid or obstruct one's access to the addiction.

(e) External Referent. Paradoxically, the disintegrating "conversion" brought about by the addiction renders the self-centered addict (or co-dependent) progressively more obsessed with the opinions and judgments of others. There is a loss of one's own real center, leading to an inability to give direction to one's life as well as a tendency to blame others for this failure.

(f) Control. As the addictive cycle progresses persons are forced to expend rapidly increasing amounts of energy controlling their addiction and the reality which so threatens it. They need to assume godlike powers to keep their life under some control and the facts of their addiction at bay.

(g) Loss of Feeling. Addicts reveal a high degree of repression concerning their feelings. Often they are completely out of touch with their emotive life, unable to handle strong feelings or to differentiate between different sorts of emotions. The addiction itself may serve as a way to block or numb one's feelings.

Types of Addiction

Several authors have spoken about two basic categories of addiction; substance and process addictions, both of which include several different types.[14]

(a) Substance Addictions (also called Ingestive Addictions) are addictions to substances, usually artificially refined or produced, that are deliberately taken into the body. These substances are almost always mood altering and lead to increased physical dependence. Some examples would be alcohol, drugs, food, nicotine and caffeine.

(b) Process Addictions are addictions in which one becomes hooked on a process—a specific series of actions or interactions. Almost all processes can be an addictive agent. Some examples include: accumulating money, gambling, sex, work, religion, worry, etc.[15]

It is important to note here that the difference between these categories is in the object or focus of one's addiction, not in the agent. Structurally both sorts operate and function in the same fashion, leading to the same conclusion.

One of the more interesting corollaries of the fact that there are so many ways in which a person may become addicted is the discovery of multiple or cross-addictions. The treatment of addicts has often been impeded by the unrecognized presence of another (or several other) addiction(s). Persons being treated for alcohol addiction may often discover in their recovery process that they were simultaneously suffering from other substance addictions, such as drugs or caffeine, or process addictions to work or sex. The primary addiction may have masked these other compulsions, which also need to be addressed if the patient is to achieve health. Failure to address these cross-addictions renders one's sobriety more tenuous and makes remission more likely. Real sobriety and sanity will depend on being willing to work progressively on all of these addictions.[16]

Levels of Addiction

Recent work in this area has made it clear how such compulsions operate on a variety of levels. Carnes and Schaef have done some interesting work on the relationship between addictive behavior in individuals and the familial systems and societal belief systems which support them.

"Personal" Addiction. The disease model employed by AA to explain alcoholism reflects an integrated grasp of the human person. Addiction is seen as a threat to the whole health of the person—in the realm of the physical, emotional, psychological and spiritual. This model refuses to accept a dualistic dichotomizing of the mind/body or body/soul which has dominated so much of our thinking in medicine about diseases and in theology about sin. Instead, the AA disease model is able to retrieve some of the biblical realism concerning an integral anthropology. A better employment of such realism in moral theology would remind us that sin is not just about the human will, intellect or immortal (and immaterial) soul, but is a profoundly personal reality which threatens the whole person with death.[17]

"Family" Addiction. Addiction, however, does not seem to work only on the personal level. The work of AA, Al Anon and many in the developing fields of substance and process addictions has shown again and again the interpersonal and familial dimensions of an addictive process which entangles spouses, lovers, parents, children, and co-workers in enmeshed, dependent, oppressive, alienating and ultimately pathological relationships. Whole family systems cooperate in an addictive process which seems to pass itself from generation to generation, being manifested by different family members in a variety of addictive and co-dependent patterns rooted in the past and bearing seeds for the yet unborn.[18]

Such an interpersonal grasp of addictions and the addictive process which distorts whole systems may give us a better tool for understanding the processes of sin which stand behind and are manifested in the specific sins or transgressions committed by individual persons. It may also help us to overcome some of the dualistic thinking about the guilty and the innocent which is so endemic to the crime model of sin, reminding us instead that we are all sinners (doctrine of original sin) and that we are all in need of the salvation Christ brings.

On this very point the most intriguing, revolutionary and perhaps upsetting work currently being done in the area of addiction concerns the question of co-dependents and/or co-addicts. The progressive realization that co-dependents too suffer from their own specific malaise, one generated by the same core addictive process which stands behind the various substance and process addictions, seriously undermines any attempt to think dualistically about addicts and non-addicts. At the same time such studies are making us aware of the pervasive character of this core process and the ways in which so many persons cooperate in it.[19]

When the insights of multiple or cross-addictions are coupled with the work being done on addictive families and co-dependents one recognizes rather swiftly that the notion of sin as a crime of transgression committed by a single individual is woefully inadequate and probably part of a larger defense system limiting our own awareness of the reality of this evil.

"Societal" Addiction. Patrick Carnes and Anne Wilson Schaef have both examined the ways in which personal addictions and addictive interpersonal systems interact with addictive processes on the societal level.[20] Carnes points out that irrational societal belief systems maintain interper-

sonal and personal addictions, while Schaef explains the relationship between individual addicts and societal compulsions about sex, money and power. Many of the same structures and oppressive relationships which characterize the pathological cycle of addiction on the personal and familial levels also evidence themselves in societal addictions. Furthermore, societies often suffer from multiple addictions, like militarism, neo-colonialism, consumerism and sexism. Such cross-addictions make the road to recovery inordinately difficult.

The Addictive Process

In her text on co-dependency Anne Wilson Schaef speaks about an "addictive process" which stands behind all the various types and levels of addiction and co-dependence. She argues that this process is intrinsic to the addictive systems operating on the familial, societal and global levels of the human community. She posits that this addictive process

> is an unhealthy and abnormal disease process, whose assumptions, beliefs, behaviors and lack of spirituality lead to a process of non-living that is progressively death-oriented. This basic disease, from which spring the subdiseases of co-dependence and alcoholism—among others—is tacitly and openly supported by the society in which we live.[21]

Schaef's assertion reflects part of a developing awareness that addictive behavior on the individual, familial and societal levels may be rooted in a fundamental "process" or reality standing behind all of these experiences.

Employing an Addiction Model for Sin

The Addiction of Sin

Now the question confronts us: In what way(s) is sin like an addiction? How may the moral illness of sin be understood as an addiction? Let me suggest a number of responses.

In its basic structure human sinfulness has been described as a twofold movement, beginning with an aversion to God.[22] In sin we struggle to supplant God, aspiring, as the addict does, to an impossible perfection and driven by delusions of grandiosity. A core element of both sin and addiction is the refusal to accept our own limitations, our own imperfections, our own creatureliness. The serpent knows well how to tempt us. We want to be godlike, but in such an awful way.

The second movement of sin has also been referred to as a conversion to some part of creation.[23] Having refused God's offer to be God, the suddenly frightened and alone sinner struggles to find a replacement in a small piece of creation. This idolatry is an addiction to that which is neither God nor life-giving. The prophets mocked such faith in clay figurines much as Thompson's hound reminds us of the vanity of finding salvation in some parcel of creation. The folly of these addictions is that "all things betrayest thee who betrayest me."

With a growing immersion in sin we experience not a gain but a loss in freedom. Sin, like addiction, seems to involve a progressive enslavement to our compulsions. The sinner continues to suffer from the illusion that the "liberty" to rebel is authentic human freedom, thinking it better to reign in hell than serve in heaven. However, the fundamental freedom to give oneself away as gift, to care about others, or to love continues to deteriorate. With the growth of sin's power the sinner becomes less able to change, grow, or repent. Instead there is a sort of hardening of the heart, a deadening of one's soul.

Sin also leads to disintegration. The sinner experiences an ongoing loss of meaning, an inability to commit oneself or give direction to one's life. Within, the self becomes a mass of contradictions. The emotional, psychological, spiritual, physical and mental integrity of the person is progressively destroyed by sin.

Sin is alienating. It systematically undermines and distorts all significant relationships. Alienation, oppression, domination and dependency replace relationships of peacefulness, harmony and justice. The sinner, like the addict, is at odds with self, with neighbor, with creation and with God. In this way sin operates as an addiction and as an addictive system by alienating the addict and distorting all the relationships around him/her.

Furthermore, sin, like all addictions, is based on and fed by lies. John reminds us how sin hates the light of truth, while Satan is called the prince of lies. Genesis gives us a haunting tale of the half-truths of the serpent along with the deceptions (hiding in the forest), denials and projections of the first couple. Anne Schaef's assertion that an addiction is anything you need to lie about could serve just as well as a litmus test for sin.

And, finally, the process of sin, paralleling the pathology of every addiction, is death-bearing. Sin leads inevitably to death, releasing all sorts of violence upon the self, the neighbor and the created order. Indeed, even the traditional language about "mortal" sin underscored the fact that authors were referring to a conversion unto death.

It would seem therefore that structurally sin operates as

an addiction in a number of ways. The sinner is like an addict—denying his/her creatureliness, refusing to let God be God, creating a delusional world through deception, denial and projection, becoming alienated from all others and destroying the self in a spiral of disintegration ending in death.

Some "Addictive" Sins

In order to put some meat on this argument it might be helpful to look at a number of sins, seeing how they operate as addictions. In line with what has been said earlier about the need to move beyond individualistic and privatizing categories of sin, we will examine four sins which impact on the personal, interpersonal and societal levels.[24] It will not be possible to show all the ways in which each of these sins operates as an addiction, but a brief sketch should illustrate their compulsive and pathological character. The four sins chosen constitute serious and deadly threats to the human community: (1) consumerism (materialism), (2) neo-colonialism, (3) militarism (the arms race), and (4) sexism.

(1) *Consumerism.* John Paul II has made it abundantly clear that he understands consumerism as a serious moral evil, an outgrowth of the idolatry of materialism and a threat to the possibility of a just global community.[25] John Kavanaugh's *Following Christ in a Consumer Society* offers a biting critique of the crass materialism which undergirds and permeates the consumer society and culture. Speaking about the idolatry of the "commodity form," Kavanaugh illustrates how consumerism replaces a life-giving God and a humane community with inanimate commodities which are worshiped and craved with a sterile passion.[26] In Kavanaugh's

analysis it is clear that the free, creative person becomes a consumer by being reduced to a one-dimensional addict, whose needs are artificially created by advertising and unsatisfactorily met by planned obsolescence. Thus, the more one has, the less one is, and the more one needs. For the consumer, like the addict, there is no such thing as enough. The cycle of hunger, empty gratification and further hunger drives the addicted consumer.

Tragically, the individual consumer is sold an addictive bill of goods by the materialist belief system which tells him/her that:

a. I am worthless without this product.
b. No one could love me without this product.
c. No living person would consistently meet my needs as well as this product would.
d. This product is my greatest need. I must have it.

This delusional belief system leads the consumer to impaired thinking, a cycle of consumption in search of happiness, and a progressively unmanageable life.

Although "binge" shopping and "plastic" substance abuse may occur in a minority of the population, the consumer ideology permeates our society. The idolatry of the commodity form has created a culture consuming inordinate and irreplaceable amounts of global resources in a way that is robbing the poor and stealing the inheritance of future generations. This same consumption is poisoning our ecosystem, destroying our personal and corporate health and triggering a mass paranoia which sees enemies everywhere and spends intolerable sums for weapons systems.[27]

In turn the consumer ideology is fed by the Orwellian "newspeak" of advertising, which tells us that real happiness

can be charged. Through advertising persons come to believe that all their disastrous imperfections ("the heartbreak
of psoriasis," or the newly discovered terror, "gingivitis")
can be remedied with a purchase, or that the measure of a
person is his/her cash value (a recent bumper sticker reads,
"The one who dies with the most toys wins"). Thus advertising articulates the consumer belief system. Indeed, it may
function as its magisterium or ministry of information.

(2) *Colonialism and Neo-Colonialism.* In *Populorum
Progressio* Paul VI severely criticized several of the basic
assertions of the contemporary western grasp of development and the so-called promise of growth held out to the
poorer nations of the world.

First, the pope argued that the opiate of steady economic growth and open trade in a competitive economy did
not reflect the current reality. Indeed, instead of being characterized by openness, mutuality, fairness and interdependence, relations between the wealthier and poorer nations of
the world were deteriorating rapidly. A "gap" was growing
between the industrialized and third world nations, progressively alienating the haves from the have-nots, rendering the
latter even poorer and more dependent upon the super-
developed nations of the north.[28] Referring to this condition
as neo-colonialism and an "imperialism of money," Paul VI
argued that the political and economic structures established
by the former colonists had placed third world nations at a
serious disadvantage in current global economic exchanges.
This was not surprising, as the dependence of such poorer
nations upon single cash crop economies had been created
by colonial powers to meet the needs of the motherland,
paying no attention to the concerns or good of local peoples.
Such dependence was being further entrenched by contemporary economic practices that limited the access of poorer

nations to industrial markets, preferring to give aid, not trade, to these nations.

Neo-colonialism represents an addictive system on a global scale. The crass one-dimensional materialism of consumerism is exported in a system which reduces whole nations to commodities and pays no attention to the persons, cultures and societies behind these products. The human family becomes the co-dependents of the addicted consumer nations that devour a superabundance of goods, burn up fossil fuels at an intolerable and poisonous rate, and construct massive propaganda and defense systems to protect their addiction (our "national interest").

Within neo-colonialism growth becomes the process addiction. Development in the western model is identified with the net growth of a nation's GNP. If there is an increase in this figure then "God's in his heaven and all's right with the world." Paul VI and John Paul II criticize this one-dimensional grasp of human development, this idolatry of the economic dimension.[29] Human development involves much more than this on either the personal or social level.

The uncritical faith placed in GNP growth ignores the fact that this increase in wealth has not solved the problems of world hunger or poverty, but has tended to put money into the pockets of the wealthy and weapons of reactionary violence into the hands of oppressors. Like all other process addictions a fixation on GNP growth has ignored disastrous side-effects, led to progressive alienation, and generally created a state worse than the first. Naturally all of this input has been ignored and GNP growth continues to be seen by many as a panacea to all human woe.

Finally, the development model of neo-colonialism is based upon the fiction that the present levels of prosperity in the west could be attained by the poor nations of the world.

Such an assertion ignores both the limited global resources which are being consumed by the west with a short-sighted vengeance and the fact that the wealth of the first world depends in large part upon the poverty of the southern hemisphere. In other words, neo-colonialism operates as an addictive system, by holding forth a promise which cannot be realized. Such promises keep the poor and the wealthy anaesthetized to the present and real situation of oppression and injustice.

(3) *Militarism.* Paul VI declared that the arms race constituted a crime against humanity and an unjustifiable offense against the poor, whose bread was stolen to pay for weapons.[30] Dr. Helen Caldicott, in her text *Missile Envy,* diagnoses the "pathological dynamics of the arms race."[31] Caldicott's critique of the arms race reveals a pathological cycle of death and denial operating on an international level and threatening the very survival of humanity.

According to her analysis the race for nuclear supremacy began with an attempt to achieve the limited good of security. Having interpreted the lesson of Germany's blitzkrieg to mean that peace can only be achieved by being prepared for war, the United States and the Soviet Union set about accumulating a warehouse of weapons. Not wanting to face Bismark's guns or butter dilemma, post-war America opted for the cheap-krieg of a nuclear arsenal. Not wanting to fall behind, the Soviets took up the race.

Unfortunately, right from the start there was a serious problem. As Einstein had noted, "The splitting of the atom has changed everything save man's mode of thinking; thus we drift toward unparalleled catastrophe." In other words, the introduction of nuclear and then thermonuclear weapons created an entire new global reality, one in which security was not enhanced but endangered with the stockpiling of bombs. Like any addiction, the arms race had initiated with an assumption that the process of accumulating nuclear weapons was the solution to the problem of war. In time, however, this process, the arms race, became problematic and counterproductive. Ultimately it came to constitute the single most serious threat to the survival of the addict and the very antithesis of global security.

Throughout this process the addicts (the United States and Russia, to name two of the worst) consistently blinded themselves to this change by engaging in the massive denials, deceptions and projections of cold war propaganda. Indeed, it would be difficult to imagine an addictive process that has involved more secrecy, deception and projection than the arms race. Probably the two single-most obvious co-addicts of the twentieth century have enabled each other's compulsion in a co-dependent system which may well lead to the death of the human family.

The process addiction of accumulating nuclear weapons is insatiable. For, truly, one 50 megaton warhead is too many and one thousand do not seem to be enough. Furthermore, the compulsion of the "superpowers" constitutes an immoral drain on human and natural resources, heightens global tensions, and generates industries of war and war-making around the world. For the weapons' addicts have been forced to become weapons' dealers to support their habit, rendering non-proliferation treaties hypocritical in the extreme.

A major part of the addictive process has been the denial involved in the suppression of feelings. It is impossible to think that a nation which had been allowed to view the carnage of Hiroshima could sit calmly by and listen to politicians and soldiers clinically discuss the surgical strikes of a limited or winnable nuclear war. Only a culture completely disconnected from its own feelings could be so dispassionate or so out of touch with the fear of annihilation.[32]

Indeed, the cool analytic calculus characteristic of the arms race may reveal not only the suppression of appropriate feelings but also Carnes' stages of preoccupation and ritualization. That is to say that the "cold" war may be a sort of nuclear foreplay.

Of some relevance here is the point the American bishops make in *The Challenge of Peace,* when they note that real peace is not simply the absence of armed conflict, but the build-up of a real harmony based upon truth, justice, equality and interdependence. Their argument shows that in the addictive process of the arms race the cold war is not recovery but a part of the "stinking thinking" of the addiction, what AA refers to as a "dry drunk".

(4) *Sexism.* The first draft of the U.S. bishops' pastoral, "Partners in the Mystery of Redemption," makes it clear that the sin of sexism permeates our culture on the personal, interpersonal and societal levels. Like every form of bigotry this sin is an offense against the sacred dignity of human persons, expressing itself in irrational beliefs, wrongful speech and acts, unjust practices and oppressive systems.[33]

Perhaps the most obvious trait of sexism, or the one which tends to offend most immediately, is oppression. By now everyone is aware of the profound injustices visited upon women in the distribution of power, money, education, and employment within our male-dominated cultures. Schaef has written about the fact that women have become the primary co-dependents in what she calls the "white male system." She argues that this is the core addictive system permeating contemporary society and that it operates within cultures just as addictions do in a dysfunctional family.[34] The white male, like the addict, becomes the controlling center of reality, forcing co-dependents to define themselves and their lives in terms of his truth or needs.[35]

In part, the oppression of sexism is rooted in the alienating ways in which males and females are taught to think of each other, disregarding the humanity of the other by transforming persons into commodities for consumption and/or threats to their survival. Carnes has pointed out that the behavior of individual addicts finds its ground in the sexist belief systems of society. But such behavior patterns are not the only fruit of this disease. Indeed, the whole sexist system, which permeates our homes, schools, churches, businesses and governments, is only able to justify such rampant injustices because of a sexist belief system which, one author has noted, trains our men to be minirapists and our women to be minimasochists.[36]

Sexism operates as an addiction. It has a faulty belief system which leads to impaired thinking processes that support the addictive abuse of human persons as commodities. It certainly has a wide system of preoccupation with and ritualization about the sexual commodity. On a systems level it is clearly oppressive, acting in a self-centered way and rendering the addict the hub of all reality. And there is no doubt but that the system is pathological, for in different ways it is squeezing the life and creativity out of both halves of the human race.

"Cross-Sins"

From the above sketches one can see the addictive character of these sins. Each includes most or all of the basic elements of the addictive cycle, operates as an addiction or addictive system on a number of levels, and tends toward disintegration and death.

What also becomes clear from a review of these and other major sins is the way in which these obsessions operate as multiple and cross-addictions. Caldicott has noted, along with many others, the ways in which the greed of American society supports its militarism.[37] She also points to the dominant role of sexism in the cancerous growth of the arms race.[38] Kavanaugh makes a large point of the relation between sexism and the commodity form of consumerism, showing how they feed each other.[39] And certainly many have noted that colonialism and militarism are two of the most ancient of allies.[40] In our global society all of these multiple addictions tend to support and reinforce one another, making the progress to sanity and sobriety a treacherous one indeed.

Advantages of an Addictive Model

By understanding the addictive character of sin we gain a more realistic grasp of human freedom. An awareness of the addictive behavioral and belief systems which permeate our social structures helps us to see how sin operates on various levels and situates personal freedom before it is engaged in conscious decisions. In this way we come to recognize that such freedom is not the either/or, guilty/innocent of the crime model but exists on a continuum in which persons are more or less free.

Such a model also explains how this admittedly contextualized freedom may be progressively lost through immersion in sin. The sinner, like the addict, becomes less and less free, more compulsive and less integral. The addiction model offers an excellent paradigm of the "conversion" process of the sinner through which a fundamental option for death is made, and from which the sinner cannot return without the grace of God.

For the notion of addiction underscores the paralyzing loss of freedom endemic to sin. Having cooperated in sin the "addict" is now in another place, a place from which return is not so simple as entry had been. The twin concepts of multiple and cross-addictions offer further illustrative evidence of the growing web into which the struggling sinner is entangled. Such concepts act as a counter to some of the naiveté characterizing the crime model of sin, naiveté which assumes that the sinner could easily enough walk away from this new and deadly context.

Furthermore, the developing awareness of addictive families and societies may well offer a key insight into understanding how sin operates on various levels, and how it is appropriate to speak about social and structural sin. This awareness was impeded by a criminal model relying exclusively upon individualistic and juridical categories of freedom. Such a model couldn't see how an impersonal society could sin or why an individual member of that society should carry guilt by association. Instead, the addiction model highlights the various ways in which the cycles and systems of addiction flourish on personal, interpersonal and societal levels.

In the same fashion this paradigm is able to offer an insight into the way in which evil communicates itself from one generation to the next, a model based upon an integral anthropology which takes seriously the physiological, psychological, social and spiritual dimensions of the human person. In such a fashion we might escape the tendency to see the origin of sin grounded in either sexual intercourse or bad example.

The development of the concepts of co-addict and co-dependent (not to be confused with one another) offers real insights into the wide variety of ways in which persons may cooperate in, be coopted by, or enable the ongoing addictions of others or themselves. The point here is not to discover a new (and larger) group of persons to "blame." Instead, these concepts make one aware of the insidious ways in which evil permeates our lives and the folly of attempting to divide the world (as the crime model does) into the guilty and the innocent.

For in the final analysis the addictive model is not about guilt and innocence. It is not juridical but therapeutic, concerned primarily not with establishing culpability, rendering judgment and assigning punishment, but with treating, healing and curing. Herein lies a fundamental strength of this particular disease model. It not only gives us a coherent way to think about sin, it also presses us beyond self-absorbed reflection into action, action which is consistent with the twin gospel calls of repentance and forgiveness.

Thus it is not at all surprising to note that most of the work on addiction only begins with analysis, moving swiftly and ultimately into therapy and action. After all, the reason that persons "study" addiction is to achieve sobriety, for themselves and/or others.

The proliferation of writings and programs on therapy provides a fertile source for reflection as well as concrete pastoral help for the "recovering" sinner. First of all, the addiction model and its "twelve step" programs offer a more realistic grasp of the process of conversion which repentance from sin involves. Any recovering addict knows well enough that detoxification is just one piece of a lifelong journey toward ever greater sobriety. The heart of sin will not be so swiftly eradicated from the human heart. Instead, conversion is a process and the sinner must always be "working the program" of his/her sobriety. This sobriety is more a verb than a noun.

Secondly, the reality of multiple and cross-addictions makes it clear that conversion will probably include a number of recovery processes. As one addiction is uncovered, confronted and worked at, other cross-addictions will surface. It will be necessary to recognize and work at each of these, steadily progressing toward a fuller and livelier sobriety. Conversion will not be a linear, but an integrative process in which the life of the recovering addict is being progressively put back together.

Also, the reality of addictive systems highlights the need to be converted on a number of levels. Personal, interpersonal and social repentance and conversion will go hand in glove, each feeding and supporting one another. Thus the task of "recovery" will need to go on in the person, the family and the society. It will not be possible to work on one of these recovery processes while ignoring or putting the others on hold.

Finally, the therapeutic approach of the "twelve steps" is profoundly (if not specifically) Christian. It invites persons and communities to surrender idolatrous fixations, accept the goodness of creation and their place in it, and make an ongoing act of faith in the loving fidelity of God and the creative splendor of life. It calls us to enter into open and trusting relationships with our God, our neighbor, creation and ourselves, to accept our creatureliness in gratitude and hope, and to reach out in love to others in pain. For the believer, addiction and recovery offer intriguing and helpful ways of understanding the mystery of sin and conversion.

Notes

1. Howard Clinebell. *Understanding and Counseling the Alcoholic* (Nashville: Abingdon, 1978) 167–178.
2. Anne Wilson Schaef, *When Society Becomes an Addict* (San Francisco: Harper and Row, 1987) 3–33. Patrick Carnes, *Out of the Shadows* (Minneapolis: CompCare, 1983) 115–132. Vernon E. Johnson, *I'll Quit Tomorrow* (New York: Harper and Row, 1973) 7–13.
3. William Lenters, *The Freedom We Crave* (Grand Rapids: William B. Eerdmans, 1985) 11–28.
4. Anne Wilson Schaef, *Co-Dependence: Misunderstood-Mistreated* (Minneapolis: Winston Press, 1986) 3–12.
5. Carnes, *Out of the Shadows*, 4–5.
6. Johnson, *I'll Quit Tomorrow*, 14–24.
7. Clinebell, *Understanding the Alcoholic*, 19–21.
8. Schaef, *When Society Becomes an Addict*, 18.
9. Carnes, *Out of the Shadows*, 1–21.
10. Johnson, in *I'll Quit Tomorrow*, chapters 2–4, shows the cycle and spiral of addiction. See also Sharon Wegscheider, *Another Chance* (Palo Alto: Science & Behavior Bks. Inc., 1981) 58–75.
11. For an analysis of intergenerational addictive systems cf. among others Michael Elkin, *Families Under the Influence* (New York: W.W. Norton & Co., 1984) chapters 1 & 2; Wegscheider, *Another Chance*, chapters 4–10; Judith Seixas and Geraldine Youcha, *Children of Alcoholism* (New York: Harper & Row, 1985). For a study of institutional violence being passed from generation to generation cf. the Medellín document on peace, especially sections 15–19; as well as Donal Dorr's *Spirituality and Justice* (Maryknoll: Orbis, 1984), chapter 4.
12. Johnson, *I'll Quit Tomorrow*, 4–5.

13. The list of characteristics has been drawn primarily from Johnson's *I'll Quit Tomorrow*, and Schaef's *When Society Becomes an Addict*, although most other texts on the subject listed all of these items in some form or another.

14. Schaef, *When Society Becomes an Addict*, 19–25; William R. Miller, *The Addictive Behaviors* (New York: Pergamon Press, 1980); Lenters, *The Freedom We Crave*, 103–111.

15. Schaef, *When Society Becomes an Addict*, 19–20.

16. Carnes, *Out of the Shadows*, 18–19; Len Sperry, "The Respectable Addictions," in *Human Development*, vol. 8, no. 4, Winter 1987, 26–30.

17. Wegscheider, *Another Chance*, 32–43.

18. *Ibid.*, 44–57, 76–88.

19. Schaef, *Co-Dependence*, 21–40.

20. Carnes, *Out of the Shadows*, 115–132; Schaef, *When Society Becomes an Addict*, 3–33.

21. Schaef, *Co-Dependence*, 21.

22. "Aversio voluntaria a Deo per conversionem illicitam ad creaturas" represents a basic grasp of sin found in Augustine, in *Contra Faustum*, XXII, 28 (PL 42, 419) as well as Thomas, *Summa Theologiae*, 1a 2ae q.87, art. 4.

23. *Ibid.*

24. Several examples of sinful behavior operating as addictions on the "personal" level are discussed in Lenter's *The Freedom We Crave*.

25. John Paul II, *Sollicitudo Rei Socialis*, 28, 31, 36–37; *Laborem Exercens*, 13, 15.

26. John Kavanaugh, *Following Christ in a Consumer Society* (Maryknoll: Orbis, 1981) 21–26.

27. John Paul II, *Sollicitudo Rei Socialis*, 22–24.

28. Paul VI, *Populorum Progressio*, 6–11; John Paul II, *Sollicitudo Rei Socialis*, 14–26.

29. Paul VI, *Populorum Progressio*, 14–21; John Paul II, *Sollicitudo Rei Socialis*, 27–30.

30. Paul VI, *Address of His Holiness Paul VI to the General Assembly of the United Nations* (October 4, 1965) 19–24; John XXIII, *Pacem in Terris*, 109–119.

31. Helen Caldicott, *Missile Envy* (New York: Bantam Books, 1986) 74–110, 229–265.

32. Caldicott, *Missile Envy*, 235–243, 247–251.

33. USCC, *Partner's in the Mystery of Redemption* (a first draft), in *Origins*, vol. 17, no. 45, April 21, 1988, 757–788.

34. Schaef, *When Society Becomes an Addict*, 33.

35. Caldicott, *Missile Envy*, 235–247.

36. Carnes, *Out of the Shadows*, 115–122.

37. Caldicott, *Missile Envy*, 265; John Paul II, *Sollicitudo Rei Socialis*, 20.

38. Caldicott, *Missile Envy*, 235–243.

39. Kavanaugh, *Following Christ in a Consumer Society*, 35–40.

40. *Medellín Documents: Peace*, 6; John Paul II, *Sollicitudo Rei Socialis*, 22.

9
·

RECOVERY FROM SIN
■   ■   ■

Recovery as a Reason for This Book

There is something a tad comic about yet another Irish-
man sitting down to pen a text on sin. Weren't the
penitentials and manuals enough? Is there no end to the fascination that Celtic moral theologians stereotypically seem to
have with sin? But aside from the humorous (and perhaps
unfair) character of those comments, this book does raise a
rather serious question: Why another text on sin?

We know the reasons that would not justify such an
effort. Books on sin ought not to be written (or read) out of
some morbid fascination with evil, a kind of moral vertigo
induced by playing the voyeur with the "heart of darkness."
Sin and evil are too serious for such games. Nor should one
write about sin only with the attempt to analyze with clinical detachment the specks in others' eyes. There is a kind
of lie in that sort of pseudo-objectivity. Worse still, the
detachment would reflect an apathy about our neighbors
struggling with sin—that kind of laying on burdens and not
lifting fingers of which Jesus was so critical. And of course,

finally, no text on sin should be written as a moral harangue. We have seen how dangerous such stone casting can be.

The point of moral theology is to help believers lead fully human and Christian lives in their pilgrimage as disciples of Jesus. It seeks to proclaim the good news of the kingdom which liberates captives from the bondage of sin and death. Moral theology is about helping people to get better. For this reason this theological medicine cannot stop with diagnostic tests and clinical lab work, simply informing patients of a serious or terminal prognosis.

For, indeed, sin itself is hardly news at all. We didn't need the gospels to tell us something was terribly amiss in the human heart or that there was murderous malice afoot in our spirit. Revelation does give us the religious meaning of this evil and thus a fuller grasp of the reality of sin, but the announcement of our sinfulness comes in the context of a proclamation of God's commitment to forgiveness ("Repent, for the kingdom of God is at hand").

Thus, ultimately, any writings in moral theology on the subject of sin must be directed toward grace. They must communicate a hope-filled vision of the liberating and graceful love of God to persons everywhere oppressed and deadened by the power of sin. That is to say that they must have a pastoral character. This is not by any means a new insight, the work of Alphonse Liguori and Bernard Häring being prime examples of this long-standing trend.

And so this book must finally move beyond an analysis of sin and begin to offer some thoughts on grace and hope if it is to be authentic to the gospel. After diagnosis and prognosis there needs to be an offer of help and a commitment to therapy, probably of a joint nature. We have spoken about the illness and addiction of sin because we believe in and are committed to a process of recovery. In the end recovery is the reason for this text.

In saying that I am suggesting that recovery is not a bad term for the process of graceful healing brought about by our cooperation with the forgiving and life-giving love of God. It is not the only possible or useful term. Latin American theologians have spoken about this process as one of liberation from the oppressive structures of sin, and clearly the addict (and the addictive society) experiences recovery as liberation. Conversion is a term used to speak about the process of turning away from sin and returning to the loving presence of God.

Admittedly, these and a number of other terms are useful in describing the process of grace in the lives of sinners and sinful communities. At the same time the notion of recovery, at least as it has been employed in describing the process of healing addictions in a variety of settings and at various levels, is capable of including a number of important elements. Recovery includes repentance, conversion, liberation, reconciliation and healing.[1] Furthermore, given my use of the addictive model of sin, recovery seems an appropriate choice to describe the work of grace. I also hope to show that it is a term which offers many insights into this process.

At the present my only concern is that the term may too easily evoke a rather personalist grasp of reality, limiting the conversion process to the realm of the individual. Hopefully the previous discussion of the addictive model has made it clear that no such limits are appropriate, and that societies and cultures as well need to recover from the poisonous effects of sin.[2]

Recovery Is a Verb

Alcoholics who are not drinking and are "working the program" refer to themselves as *recovering*. One gets a sense in that verb that their recovery is an ongoing and vital part of their life. They are not just avoiding the drink, they are actively working at getting better, healthier, more whole. And they will tell you that if they stop working at their recovery they will begin to get sick again. For them living is recovery and recovery is living.

To speak then about grace as recovery is to underscore that the gift of God's healing presence is a verb in the life of persons. Too often in our grasp of sin as a stain or crime reality has been divided into the ones who were sinning and the ones who were not, as if grace was simply the absence of sin. There was a strong sense that sin was a verb, that it had a dynamic (or, perhaps better, destructive) character, while grace or goodness was a state of being untouched or un-scathed by moral evil. Grace was a kind of nothingness de-fined against the reality of sin in the same way that health was often understood as the absence of sickness.[3]

To say that I am a recovering sinner, however, creates another image entirely. Here the dynamic and life-giving character of grace is revealed. Here grace is a verb, a verb that breathes and works and prays and hopes and grows and changes. Such grace is not sterile but fertile. It gives life. The recovering sinner is progressively untying the knots and bonds, undoing the harm, and clearing out the dark corners of sin. Recovery is an experience of getting better, getting freer, getting healthier, getting reconciled.

Indeed, if addiction is a pathological relationship with a non-living substance, it makes sense to say that recovery is a vital and dynamic relationship with life itself, even that recovery is life and that grace is recovery. Thus the notion of being animated and reconciled by the life-giving love of God might be better described as recovery than as the *state* of grace.

Recovery Is a Life-long Process

What do you say to a wide-eyed youngster fresh from a personal experience of conversion who asks if you've been saved (or, better yet, to name the date on which you were saved)? "Saved" (in the perfect tense) sounds so finished, so done, so wrapped up and put away to those of us still in the midst of life. Without being glib, one is tempted to quote Yogi Berra's comment that "it ain't over till it's over." AA members introduce themselves as recovering, not recovered alcoholics, and there is an insight there worth pursuing.

Recovery from sin is a process, a lifelong process. It fills all the days of our lives, from the cradle to the grave. While there may be moments when the struggle is not so difficult, there is no early finish for anyone. The biographies of the saints (canonized or not) reveal their pilgrim's progress—being called again and again to "come up higher," to take up other tasks and challenges, to grow in other ways. The liberation of persons and cultures is a work in progress, with each step raising our consciousness higher and higher in the recognition of human dignity. The work of recovery is like the work of breathing, ongoing and steady to the very end.

Such a process will necessarily involve the stop and go of normal traffic. There will be setbacks and restarts, times when movement seems easy and others when the progress seems deadly slow or even non-existent. Thus, recovery will mean patience and forgiveness in response to our own weakness and the imperfections of others, a patience which is hopeful in the face of sometimes overwhelming difficulties. Even when things go well and we seem to achieve our immediate goals, there will be times when we come like the bear to the top of our mountain only to see other hills that need to be climbed. Becoming freed and liberated from one sinful habit or prejudice will often enough open up a porthole through which we can see other ways in which we need to grow.

At the same time the process is not all challenge or the product of our own sweat. There is a progressive liberation and encouragement, an ongoing empowerment which invites and transforms us by stages or in different branches toward a self that is more whole, more free, more Christ. For the process of recovery is ultimately a gift, a gracious and unmerited offer of God's healing and redemptive love.

Recovery Is Integration

If recovery is the work in progress of living, then the work of recovery is integration. Recovery that includes only one dimension or stage of the person's (or society's) health eventually becomes mere maintenance, then stagnation, and eventually moves toward deterioration. We are multi-faceted persons and cultures. Repair in one area often enough leads us to address other concerns which had until recently gone unnoticed.

Let us use an example. Dave, a middle-aged salesman, has just gotten a little shock therapy from his doctor. Unless he loses sixty to seventy pounds and drops his blood pressure twenty points or more he can forget about living to retirement. Frightened by this warning, Dave makes some immediate changes in his life. He needs to cut back on his food intake, cut out tobacco and drop the level of his alcohol consumption. So he starts to diet and stops smoking.

Unfortunately, withdrawal from alcohol and tobacco have made him too edgy to sleep well, and he finds it hard not to snack while sitting in front of the TV at night. As a solution he asks his wife Joan to go for a walk with him each evening, getting him away from the beer and pretzels as well as tiring him out so he can sleep better.

Their evening walks soon become a regular event and the couple find themselves out for an hour or two each night. Once they can walk comfortably without huffing and puffing the two of them begin to talk to each other about their respective days. There is a certain awkwardness at first as they find themselves getting reacquainted after years of silence before the TV or cacophony over the crowded dining room table. They begin slowly to speak openly and honestly to each other about their lives, hopes and fears. There is a kind of recovery in place.

Meanwhile Dave discovers that it is not only his diet, exercise and sleeping patterns that he needs to change. The long talks with Joan have made him aware of the stress he continuously puts himself under at work and the distance he has developed in so many relationships. He needs to think about these things and take some steps. He finds himself asking questions about the meaning and direction of his life, and wondering where to turn to find answers. He begins to look for a place for reflection and prayer in his life, perhaps deciding to go on a retreat.

During their evening walks Dave also has a chance to notice how his town has changed over the years, how crowding and unemployment and pollution have affected his environment and the environment of his children. What good will it do him to clear the cholesterol out of his heart valves if there is so much poison in the air and water and soil? He finds himself reading articles and small books on toxic waste and acid rain, keeping abreast of current legislation and reflecting on candidates in light of their voting record.

His long walks with Joan have also raised some questions about their relationship and about his understanding of her identity as a woman and a person. They wonder together about what is important to them and what they want out of life. As a result of some of these reflections they decide to make some tentative changes, simplifying their lifestyle and giving some time to community services.

This story is rather simplistic (and may reflect a liberal democrat agenda), but its point is that the healing of recovery moves steadily toward inclusion of the whole human experience. Recovery is organic, constantly working toward fuller and fuller integration. Recovery includes the mind, the body, the emotions, and the spirit of human beings. It also includes the reconciling of persons, families and nations, the healing of familial, societal and ecological wounds, as well as the sinful rift between humanity and God.

For sin is a pathological reality permeating the whole of human experience, and so recovery needs to work at fixing all of the pieces and progressively putting them all back together. Through stages and in different branches the work of recovery is a mending task, knitting the torn pieces back into a quilt. Fixing one piece leads to strengthening and repairing another.

But recovery is not just about patching the various dimensions of our lives back together. It is also about sorting out the chaos and confusion our lives have become as a result of the web of our various sins. For it might be said that the integrative process of recovery often moves in stops and starts because it is like the old children's game of "pick-up-sticks." The jumble of sticks represents the ways in which the various types of sin act as cross-addictions, frustrating easy progress. To move very far in any one direction it will be necessary to sort out not only one issue but a number of concerns. Recovery then is the process by which we untie the multiple knots and webs of our cross-addictive sins and progressively integrate ourselves into a new reality.

Recovery in and of Community

Nor, as we have noted, does this integration take place only on the level of the individual person. For two concepts continue to surface throughout the process of recovery in the twin shorthand phrases of "not God" and "not alone." They are fundamental to the notion of recovery, for they speak about the profoundly communitarian character of this life-giving process, as well as the fact that recovery is a gift.

The road out of the heart of darkness begins with a cry for help, but that cry will only be raised if one believes there is someone there to hear it. Recovery begins with a recognition that the help which I so desperately need is available. I am not alone. The profoundest expression of this not-aloneness is the realization that I am not (and do not need to be) God. There already is a God.

With that realization it is possible then to do all sorts of wonderful things, not the least of which is relax. It is possible to recognize my own limits and creatureliness, realities which need not terrify me as long as there is a God. It is possible to trust this God enough to ask for help. It is even possible to hand control of my life over to this God. This does not mean abandoning responsibility, but contextualizing that responsibility by cutting its dimensions to human proportions.

Recovery in the recognition that one is "not God" means living in trust and letting go of those elements of our reality over which we have no real control at all. Recovery means the loss of useless and death-dealing worries. Recovery means self-acceptance, forgiveness and peace.

The second dimension of that not-aloneness of recovery is the recognition of our neighbor (personal and global) and world. Recovery involves a progressive reconciliation with others, an undoing of hurts and a binding up of old wounds. Recovery is the building up of the true peace of the community of whole persons, a peace constructed on truth, openness, charity and justice.

At the same time recovery involves the support and help of others, for no one recovers alone. Recovery depends on the simple honesty of confrontation, the loving support of encouragement, the attentive listening ear and the mending hands of forgiveness. Recovery does not just call me to reach out of myself, it calls me to reach for others. Recovery is creative. It creates "us" where there was you and I and they. Further, the work of recovery is one of continuous integration, one that is always recognizing anew the need to tear down walls and create larger communities.

Finally, the "not-aloneness" of recovery is a reminder that no one is already recovered. There is no completion to personal recovery while the community is being built. Every person (and, indeed, every culture) is in continual need of ongoing recovery.

The Recovering Personality

In the integrating process of recovery disparate bits and pieces are progressively rewoven into the fabric of a whole person (or a just society), overcoming the chaos and madness of addiction and creating a new personality. While no two recovering persons are alike (and certainly not identical), there are some basic character traits of the recovering sinner which tend to show up again and again.

Life-Affirming. Recovery is life-affirming, while evil and addiction are drawn ever deeper into the gray monotony of the dead. In recovery there is a consistent decision to affirm life in all of its vitality, complexity, vibrancy and difficulties. In its affirmation of life recovery is willing to take risks, to suffer pain, to undergo tremendous changes, to surrender attachments to all sorts of stable crutches. Recovery is willing to engage all the trials and difficulties, challenges and dangers, failures and frustrations that confront us as we breathe in and breathe out several thousand times a day.

For this reason it is right to say that recovery is hopeful, for it is clearly not fearful or despairing. Recovery has a certain courage and trust, a profound openness to the reality of the present moment as well as a commitment to the long haul.

Honest. Recovery also entails a commitment to the truth. For much of the process of recovery involves tearing down the webs and shadows of one's (or one's society's) illusions and deceptions. The madness of sin has been in the myriad of lies that have been told and need continuously to be fabricated in order to sustain earlier ones. Recovery is a process of honesty, of simple speech and of single-minded dedication to the truth. The process of recovery recognizes that the emperor has no clothes, or perhaps that the emperor has no business buying so many new clothes while his people are naked. Recovery is willing to ask probing and critical questions of belief systems and ideologies. There are no sacred cows in recovery. Instead, there is a profound kind of poverty required for a real commitment to the truth.

Recovery then is particularly concerned with the elimination of lies, propaganda and those secrets which divide the community and protect vested interests, or attempt to "keep the peace" by not telling the truth or not playing fair. Recovery can therefore be confrontational, including a sometimes painful consciousness-raising process. But recovery is not cruel, nitpicking or vicious. Instead, it is simple and honest, sometimes painfully but never brutally so.

Holistic. Recovery is well centered, with a strong sense of the self and community. In the process of recovery the ego (and the nation state) needs less and less the huge defense systems and inflated self-concepts that create a barrage keeping so many at bay. There is a growing sense of acceptance of the self, with all the limits and forgiveness that involves. Recovery moves the self away from a paranoid state of blame and defense into one of peace.

The centering of recovery is also transpersonal, pulling the self beyond the boundaries of its own ego (or the borders of its national interest). In recovery we learn to pay appropriate and loving attention to others, to respect them without being swallowed up by our need to be approved of by them. Recovery moves beyond narcissism without becoming self-annihilation or co-dependence. It is about a healthy sense of mutuality, interdependence and love. Indeed, a fundamental meaning of recovery is love, for it involves a deep and abiding love of God, the neighbor, the self and all created reality.

Some Conclusions

This book began with the discussion of a crisis, one of both theory and praxis. As a first step in responding to that crisis I have suggested that there was a need to replace (or at least augment) traditional images of human sinfulness with some different models, and I have gone on to suggest that an excellent corrective and contribution might be made by shifting toward a model of addiction and recovery as a way of explaining sin and grace.

Having briefly explained these models, the question arises as to how their incorporation will or should affect our practice concerning sin. That is, how will such models impact on the ways we preach about sin, confess sin, and overcome the power of sin in our lives? It is to these questions that we now turn.

Preaching on Sin: Yes and No

Karl Menninger wrote his text on sin at least in part for the express purpose of calling preachers to speak about sin—a strange notion for a physician who has written often and critically about the punitive and guilt-inducing character of society. But Menninger, while rejecting moralistic harangues which seek to lay on burdens, is also aware of the dangerous "sounds of silence" on this topic.[4]

For sin does not disappear when we refuse to speak about it. Instead, our conspiracy of silence gives sin a greater power. It becomes an invisible and unmentionable reality in our lives, a shadow looming ever larger on our consciousness, a crescendoing rhythm beating a tattoo in the background of our hearts and minds. Our silence renders our sins the black holes of our universe, around which we must continually and cautiously skirt. In the end our silence is more work and more deadly than addressing the issue.

But sin, as we know, does not want to be addressed or

named. It hates the light of day. It hates the truth. And it
frightens us with that hate. The message of sin that intimi-
dates us into silence is that if we do name it, if we do awaken
the monster by calling its name, things will only be worse.
There is a scent of despair in our silence, a rotting fear that
tells us sin is too big, it cannot be faced or challenged. It can
only be awakened and provoked like some sleeping dragon
which will consume us in its rage. Sin warns us to maintain
our shadowy silence, to wander aimlessly in an unmarked
land of vague generalities, pestered by a growing sense of
unease, but unwilling to name or confront it, victims of our
own muteness.

Or perhaps our silence on sin is also grounded in our
vested interests. Speaking concretely about our sinfulness
will heighten our own consciousness and force us to take
responsible action, to make moves involving real change in
our lives. There are ways in which we have grown comfortable with and accustomed to our sinfulness, and if many do
not desire to preach or hear sermons about particular sins it
could well be that our resistance is not disinterested. I am
less likely to recognize the sinfulness of actions, attitudes,
habits or social patterns which make my life comfortable and
the removal of which would cost me serious pain.

And so we need to preach and to be preached to on sin.
Especially within the walls of our churches we must raise our
voices and name our sins. We do this first of all as an act of
faith in the power of God's loving grace. For if we are afraid
to mention sin in the shadow of our sanctuaries or the heart
of our worship, then our faith in God is weak indeed. We
need to preach about sin as a proclamation that this monster
can be named and faced and overcome. We need to preach
as a sign against the silent despair urging us to muteness.
And we need to preach as an expression of our faith in the

mercy of God. In naming my sin before God I am not destroyed by the power of sin or the wrath of God. In confessing my sin I am confessing my faith.

Preaching on sin is also a necessary part of the confrontation which leads to liberation and reconciliation. We must first be willing to be truthful and to suffer the pain of that honesty. Preaching on sin and on our concrete sins is an integral element of the process of recovery, the unmasking of our self-deceptions, the dismantling of our systems of denial, and the shattering of our projections. Good preaching on sin lights a candle in the dark and holds up an honest mirror to our hearts, lives, families and social structures. For this reason good preaching on sin will be painful, confrontative and often as searing as a two-edged sword.

At the same time the very act of preaching on sin in a faith context can be very empowering. The frank and honest recognition of our sins and of the power of sin in our lives can open us to the call to conversion, move us to ask for forgiveness, and enable us to seek reconciliation. Naming sins can be a catalyst to real transformation. This is all the more so because good preaching on sin always takes place in the context of grace, and is itself a kind of preaching on grace, a proclamation of the good news.

Fortunately or unfortunately, the only persons or institutions available to do the work of preaching about sin are themselves infected with sin. This means that the preaching is always being done by sinners. Far from leading us to despair or cynicism, the realization that our church and our preachers are wounded healers gives us an insight into the way such preaching should take place, i.e. with humility and simplicity. Aware of the power of sin in our lives and communities we are empowered to take this reality with ultimate seriousness and address it directly. Aware of the power of grace that liberates us, we preach on sin in the context of our faith.

The best preaching on sin comes not just from sinners but from a recovering sinner. All of us, aware of it or not, are sinners; and all of us, whether we are dealing with them or not, have concrete sins in our lives. Excellent preaching on sin comes from those who are aware of their own sinfulness in at least some of its serious and specific manifestations and are attempting to "work the program" of grace in these areas. This does not mean that preaching is simply self-disclosure or self-absorption. No, real preaching is proclamation and christocentric. Nevertheless, good preaching is from a "fellow leper" proclaiming the experience of grace as liberation, reconciliation, conversion and redemption.

Such "recovering" sinners will never preach abstractly about sin or grace. Nor are they likely to preach in a way that focuses exclusively on our sins, succeeding only in raising the level of our guilt and leading us into despair. Nor will such preaching know anything about dualism between the innocent (preacher) and the guilty (congregation). Instead, such preaching will amount to a sort of shared faith proclamation that empowers us to believe in the mercy of God and enables us to put ourselves at risk in an expression of that faith. Such preaching will allow us to die to sin and be born again in the grace of Christ.

Confessing Sin

Recognizing the addictive character of sin and the recovery process of grace has a number of implications for the way in which we confess and celebrate the forgiveness of our sinfulness. These models call us to construct our liturgical practices in ways that pay increased attention to the "story" of sinners and sinful communities as well as to the life-giving power of God's gracious love.

For the past twenty-five years we have heard many a talk on reconciliation urging us to abandon a simple "grocery list" approach to confessing our sins. In an attempt to move us beyond a taboo scrupulosity which focused exclusively on the infractions we committed against God's laws, religious authors called us to look into our hearts and examine the character of our relationship with the Lord. This shift from act to person was an important step in recovering a fuller grasp of sin and grace.

At the same time there is a real need in the context of our sacramental celebrations of reconciliation to examine the story of our lives as we continue to cooperate with the Lord's grace in our ongoing recovery. For each sacramental celebration of reconciliation is also part of a lifelong process of being liberated from the power of sin, a piece of work in progress of our recovery, of our pilgrimage as disciples.

This examination of our story might take any of a number of forms. We could be invited or called to celebrate the sacrament in conjunction with a journal. This would not mean repeating each time old offenses, but getting a sense of where we are in the story of our lives by reviewing the course of our stumblings and our growths. It could also mean incorporating the practice of an annual general confession, so as to place oneself in a context where the grace of the sacrament could address the direction of our lives. It would almost certainly mean attempting to move toward a regular confessor, so that we are trusting the sacrament not only with episodic events in our lives but also with the totality of our lives.

Taking our story seriously might also lead to attempts to structure celebrations of reconciliation and forgiveness for intergenerational experiences of sin. While baptism addresses the experience and reality of original sin, many persons come only in adulthood to recognize and confront the power of sins committed against them as children, sins which they often enough find themselves committing against the next generation. Victims of abuse, violence and abandonment need not only healing but also reconciliation and experiences of forgiveness. All too often the very trajectory of our lives has been profoundly affected by actions which are unmentionable and unrecognized in our lives. The process of recovery will mean integration and reconciliation for the successive generations of victims.

But the story of sin is not mine alone. Indeed the story of my own sin isn't even just mine but one thread woven into the fabric of a community. None of us are original sinners and none of us recover alone. That certainly has implications for our worship and praxis.

While admitting the necessary, real and important place which individual reconciliation has in the life of the church, there is room for richer communitarian celebrations of forgiveness and reconciliation than are currently in practice. A couple of suggestions might surface from the examination of the support groups employed by AA and other recovery programs. The telling of such stories is a form of reconciliation with the self and with others, a way of experiencing the forgiveness of a community which is not mediated by one person alone. Such story-telling is also a form of faith sharing which empowers others to move toward forgiveness and reconciliation.

Such support groups and story-telling seem integral to the ongoing work of recovery. The shared commitment of such groups establishes a foundation upon which trust in the Lord can grow and flourish. They are havens for recovery.

Indeed, these groups have proven themselves so powerful and effective as tools in the healing process of recovery that nearly every organization dealing with persons or families struggling with addictions, dysfunctions, old wounds or dependencies have urged a long-term commitment to such group work. Certainly there ought to be a way for the church's celebration of God's ongoing reconciling love to incorporate such an approach.

Also, one might consider whether or not such sharing and support wouldn't be a good corrective for many who experience the shadowy privacy of the confessional box as reinforcing their sense of shame. The shift to face-to-face confessions in the well-lit reconciliation room was one step in this direction. Perhaps communal story-telling would be another.

At the same time the work being done in family therapy suggests that there is a need to be involved in reconciliation experiences which address the divisions within the community itself. Real reconciliation calls for not only the separate confessions of husband and wife or parents and children, but also some form of communal reconciliation. It is insufficient for the priest who has heard the confessions of several family members to encourage them individually to deal with each other better. Group reconciliation would be a better way to deal with these sorts of issues, and so there needs to be a way for believers to do that in a context where they are aware of its grace dimension. The church needs to experiment with "blessing" more communal forms of reconciliation. This would be a real way to celebrate communal forms of reconciliation in a parish or diocese, i.e. addressing the issues that divide this community. Indeed, it might even be appropriate to deal with some of the ways in which the "family" of the church has sinned against its "children."

Communal reconciliation needs also to deal with issues that are larger than the local celebrating community. An international church must work for the reconciliation of all its members and communities. Recovery must be global. To this end the work of peace, ecumenism and ecology are a few of the reconciliation issues to be addressed by a planetary church.

Recovering from Sin

Recovering means that life is given over to "working the program." It means that being alive and open to the grace of God involves a constant process of untying knots, tearing down walls, binding up wounds, as well as accepting love, forgiveness and support. Working this program includes five basic notions: prayer, honesty, love, solidarity and hope.

Prayer. The process of recovery begins and ends with God's grace. From the first haunting call to repentance we are invited to let God be God and to accept God's love and support. Prayer, whether petition, praise, thanks or anguish, is the pulse of that acceptance. It is the centering which not only places us in the presence of God but which rightly centers us in our own joyous place in creation. Prayer is the breathing exercise of recovery, the constant act of our faith in God and acceptance of ourselves. Prayer is also the pulse of God's love pumping the life-blood of grace into us. Recovery without prayer is impossible. Prayer that does not lead to recovery is unimaginable.

Honesty. The heart of sin is the lie. It is certainly the heart of addiction. Recovery demands an unconditional commitment to the truth and to honesty. Working the program of grace involves a progressive dismantling of the webs of deceptions, denials and projections of sin. Recovery demands a constant commitment to critical self-examination and to a hermeneutic of suspicion with regard to all forms of propaganda and ideologies. But it also demands a commitment to dealing with the real issues, and dealing with them in ways that do not involve exaggerations or cloud discussions with accusations loaded with hostility. A commitment to honesty in recovery is also a commitment to faithfulness.

Love. The lie of sin distorts and destroys community, tears down bridges and leaves us in not so splendid isolation. Alienation and enemy-making is a direct consequence of the sinful process. Recovery, on the other hand, is the rebuilding of those bridges, the reintegration of our lives and communities, the patchwork of a new common quilt. The work of recovery demands an ongoing practice of forgiveness and reconciliation as well as a stand in solidarity with all other fellow sinners. This means that love is essential to recovery. Indeed it is both a motive and a result of recovery.

Such love, however, must be both concrete and universal. It is too easy to love in the abstract or "spiritual" dimension. Real love must embrace the limited and frail human beings whom we are and with whom we live and work and play. Such love must be patient and forgiving with persons who require real patience and forgiveness. Such love must also take concrete actions expressing a solidarity which is more than sentiment. This love must take specific and helpful steps to care for ourselves and others. And finally such love needs to be without boundaries. There must be a profound openness within us to reach out to all persons, to break down every barrier and to forgive every offense. A commitment to recovery demands that there be this willingness to be reconciled with all persons.

Solidarity. There is no going it alone in recovery. There

never has been. There never will be. Right from the very beginning it has not been good for us to be alone. For we are not attempting to recover only that part of ourselves which is individual. We are trying to recover the wholeness of the self which is also a child of God and sibling of every other person. Good recovery means cooperation, encounter, engagement and solidarity with others. This is true not only because we need the support of others in this work, which we surely do, or even because others are a sacramental presence of God's gracious love in our lives, which they clearly are. The process of recovery requires solidarity because the goal of recovery is solidarity in a life-giving community of whole and integral persons. We are made in the image and likeness of God, a God who is community and love. To recover our full and real selves is to recover our community. Recovery involves reunion.

Hope. "Every day it's the same old thing—breathe, breathe, breathe." Stop breathing and we die; breathe and we are (only) alive. Working the program of recovery and overcoming the power of sin in our lives is not an event or moment, though it will include all the events and moments of our lives and the lives that came before and will follow after us. Recovering sinners are in this moment breathing the air of grace, cooperating in the life-giving work of recovery. They are taking one day (even moment) at a time. Whether struggling with the power of sin in personal habits or in international economic structures, they are attempting to do what can be done in cooperation with the grace and power of God.

In this way recovery avoids a number of serious and sinful pitfalls. To begin with it escapes that old self-annihilating idolatrous fiend, perfectionism. Recovery refuses to confuse the self with God or one's plans with ultimate salvation. Recovery struggles to cooperate with the grace of God while accepting the inevitable frustrations and limits up against which we continually run. This does not mean that recovery is passive, only that it is not idolatrous or despairing.

All the same recovery is forever unsatisfied. The work of recovery is ever incomplete, and so recovering sinners are constantly open to new growth and change in their lives and communities. The acceptance of our creatureliness does not call us to be content, but to live in trust as we seek to be about the work God gives us.

In all of this recovery means a kind of patience that is hopeful and a kind of hope that is patient. The recovering sinner hopes in a way that struggles to make God's transforming love more present in the world while not confusing these efforts with God or salvation. And the recovering sinner is patient with human limits and imperfections in a way that never abandons hope or embraces despair. Recovering sinners keep breathing and breathing sinners keep recovering.

Notes

1. A review of the Twelve Steps and Twelve Traditions of AA highlights the truth of the assertion that recovery includes all of these elements.

2. James Hug, S.J., "Social Sin: Cultural Healing," *Chicago Studies* 23:3 (November 1984) 333–51.

3. Rollo May's text, *Power and Innocence,* offers an interesting development of this very passive notion of goodness as an innocence which is merely the absence of life or experience. There is neither power nor vitality in such innocence.

4. Karl Menninger, *Whatever Became of Sin?* pp. 192–203.